W9-CKK-309

The
End(s)
of Ethnography

SOCIOLOGICAL OBSERVATIONS

Series Editor: **JOHN M. JOHNSON**, Arizona State University

"This series seeks its inspiration primarily from its subject matter and the nature of its observational setting. It draws on all academic disciplines and a wide variety of theoretical and methodological perspectives. The series has a commitment to substantive problems and issues and favors research and analysis which seek to blend actual observations of human actions in daily life with broader theoretical, comparative, and historical perspectives. SOCIOLOGICAL OBSERVATIONS aims to use all of our available intellectual resources to better understand all facets of human experience and the nature of our society."

—John M. Johnson

Volumes in this series:

1. **THE NUDE BEACH**, by Jack D. Douglas and Paul K. Rasmussen, with Carol Ann Flanagan
2. **SEEKING SPIRITUAL MEANING**, by Joseph Damrell
3. **THE SILENT COMMUNITY**, by Edward William Delph
4. **CROWDS AND RIOTS**, by Sam Wright
5. **THE MAD GENIUS CONTROVERSY**, by George Becker
6. **AMATEURS**, by Robert A. Stebbins
7. **CARETAKERS**, by David R. Buckholdt and Jaber F. Gubrium
8. **HARD HATS**, by Jeffrey W. Riemer
9. **LOVE AND COMMITMENT**, by Gary Schwartz and Don Merten, with Fran Behan and Allyne Rosenthal
10. **OUTSIDERS IN A HEARING WORLD**, by Paul C. Higgins
11. **MOMENTUM**, by Peter Adler
12. **WORLDS OF FRIENDSHIP**, by Robert R. Bell
13. **CHRONIC PAIN**, by Joseph A. Kotarba
14. **INVISIBLE LIVES**, by David R. Unruh
15. **SOCIAL ROLES**, by Louis A. Zurcher
16. **THE REHABILITATION DETECTIVES**, by Paul C. Higgins
17. **AGING CRIMINALS**, by Neal Shover
18. **THE ALCOHOLIC SELF**, by Norman K. Denzin
19. **THE RECOVERING ALCOHOLIC**, by Norman K. Denzin
20. **LOVE, INTIMACY, AND SEX**, by Jack D. Douglas and Freda Cruse Atwell, with John Hillebrand
21. **THE END(S) OF ETHNOGRAPHY**, by Patricia Ticineto Clough

The End(s)
of Ethnography
From Realism
to Social Criticism

Patricia Ticineto Clough

SAGE Publications
International Educational and Professional Publisher
Newbury Park   London   New Delhi

Copyright © 1992 by Sage Publications, Inc.

All rights reserved. No part of this book may be reproduced or utilized in any form or by any means, electronic or mechanical, including photocopying, recording, or by any information storage and retrieval system, without permission in writing from the publisher.

For information address:

SAGE Publications, Inc.
2455 Teller Road
Newbury Park, California 91320

SAGE Publications Ltd.
6 Bonhill Street
London EC2A 4PU
United Kingdom

SAGE Publications India Pvt. Ltd.
M-32 Market
Greater Kailash I
New Delhi 110 048 India

Printed in the United States of America

Library of Congress Cataloging-in-Publication Data

Clough, Patricia Ticineto, 1945-
    The end(s) of ethnography : from realism to social criticism/
Patricia Ticineto Clough.
        p. cm. —(Sociological observations ; 21)
    Includes bibliographical references and index.
    ISBN 0-8039-4630-9. —ISBN 0-8039-4631-7 (pbk.)
    1. Ethnology—Methodology. 2. Ethnology—Authorship.
3. Sociology—Methodology. I. Title II. Series.
GN345.C55   1992
305.8'001—dc20   92-8651

92 93 94 95 10 9 8 7 6 5 4 3 2 1

Sage Production Editor: Chiara C. Huddleston

For Christopher

plus que les ètoiles . . .

CONTENTS

Acknowledgments   ix

Preface   xi

Introduction: Writing Technologies of the Subject—
From Narrative to Narrativity   1

1. Ethnographic Authority and
   the Oedipal Logic of Realist Narrativity   15

2. Herbert Blumer: A Methodology for Writing Observation   29

3. The Figure of the Woman in the Naturalist Machine   46

4. Howard S. Becker: The Methodology
   of a Writing Observed   62

5. Steven Spielberg's Production of
   the Miniaturization of Man   80

6. Erving Goffman: Writing the End of Ethnography   94

7. Toni Morrison: Rememory and Writing   113

Concluding Remarks:
Social Criticism Beyond Ethnographic Realism   131

Index   139

About the Author   143

ACKNOWLEDGMENTS

The publication of this book offers me the opportunity to express gratitude to those who have long offered me their support and encouragement. I would especially like to thank my family: my parents, Felix and Josephine Ticineto, for their endless generosity but even more for their passion and joy in living, and my sister, Virginia Steppe, and her family for their kindness and care. I give thanks to those friends who nurtured my dreams and my hopes: my dearest and most cherished friend, Barbara Heyl, and also Ann Galligan, Anne Golomb Hoffman, Nicole Fermon, Barry Goldberg, Ellyn Rosenthal, Michal McCall, Joseph Schneider, Mary Zey, Charles Powers, Howie Becker, Elizabeth Harriss, Anahid Kassabian, Vincent Barry, Thomas McDonald, Paul Patton, Paul Hopper, and Judy Wittner. I heartily thank my teachers, whose ideas I return to again and again: first among them, Norman K. Denzin, also Heinz von Foerster, Humberto Maturano, Herbert Brun, and Gayatri Chakravorty Spivak. I am most grateful to those who gave special attention to ensure the publication of this book, especially Charles Lemert, and also Stanley Aronowitz, Norman Denzin, and John Johnson. I am indebted to Fordham University at Lincoln Center and the Society for the Study of Symbolic Interaction for their support.

Finally, I send my warmest regards to those whose words again and again bring me to tears and laughter, stirring in me the desire to write: cybernetician Paul Pangaro, Miltonist and literary theorist Marshall Grossman, poet and sociologist Zali Gurevitch, psychoanalyst Jill Herbert, and my son, Christopher Clough, to whom this book is lovingly dedicated.

PREFACE

When I began planning this book in 1986, I imagined it as an exploration of the possible impact of poststructuralist thought on the empirical social sciences, sociology in particular. At that time, poststructuralism was already having a profound influence on literary studies, cultural studies, feminist studies, and film and television studies. However, with some few exceptions, sociologists seemed yet unable to make much sense of the so-called crisis of representation and the deconstruction of the subject, both of which follow in the wake of poststructural accounts of discourse and representation.

While the 1983 publication of James Clifford's essay on ethnographic realism did lead to a more general criticism of anthropological discourse, sociologists, even those receptive to discursive and textual criticisms, seemed unable to extend the criticism of ethnographic writing to a more general criticism of sociological discourse. Perhaps this is because in sociology, the ethnographic tradition is identified with qualitative or participant observational methodologies, which are usually treated as marginal to the dominant form of quantitative or statistical sociological analysis. It seemed to me in 1986, as it does now, that if the ethnographic tradition is to be the focus of a poststructural criticism of sociology or empirical social scientific discourse generally, then the way ethnography has functioned in the construction of the authority of empirical social scientific discourse, sociology in particular, must be made more visible. Thus the aim of this book is a critical reading of the ethnographic tradition in sociology that explores the way ethnographic writing functions in the construction of the authority of sociological discourse.

But while the criticism of ethnography within anthropology has focused on the narrative production of empirical scientific authority through the form of realism that the ethnography shares with the novel, a critical reading of the ethnographic tradition in sociological discourse, I would propose, demands an understanding of the narrative production of authority not only in terms of the realist narrativity of the novel, but also in terms of the realist narrativities developed since the novel, in cinema, television, and computerized simulation. Therefore, I will argue that the forms of realist narrativity are specific to the mass media communication technologies that enframe them, and that the ethnographic tradition in sociology has been the site at which these forms of realist narrativity have been articulated for sociological discourse in an effort to maintain empiricism as the authorized form of sociological understanding and social criticism as well.

What follows, then, is a poststructural criticism of sociological discourse that elaborates its forms of realism in terms of its ethnographic tradition and the mass media communication technologies that the tradition inscribes. I hope thereby to demonstrate to sociologists the necessity of their becoming more fully engaged with the critical approaches to culture that poststructuralism now informs, not only to enable a self-criticism of sociological discourse, but also to turn that self-criticism toward the construction of a social criticism of the mass-mediated cultures for which sociological discourse has engendered and does engender authority.

Therefore, I also hope to encourage cultural critics to become engaged in rereadings of sociological discourse in order to explicate how various mass media communication technologies are enlisted in maintaining empiricism as the hegemonic form of sociological understanding and social criticism as well. This is especially important now because cultural critics have begun to turn to ethnography as a way to counter textual and discursive analyses of mass media productions, or at least as a way to supplement these analyses with empirical studies of audience response. It is important, then, that cultural critics come to understand not only that ethnography is profoundly dependent on textual forms, forms of realist narrativity, but that these forms are the very ones that cultural critics themselves have uncovered in their textual and discursive analyses of the relationship of narrativity, unconscious sexual desire, and the fictional (or, better, the fantasmatic) production of authority.

I will argue that it is precisely because empirical social science can never offer unmediated understandings of the real that its authority is, like that of the mass media with which it shares forms of realist narrativity, a production of projected or displaced unconscious sexual desire.

Thus the poststructural analysis of sociological discourse that I am proposing is informed with both psychoanalytic and feminist orientations. These orientations carry my desire to engage what I will describe as crucial to the fantasmatic production of authority in realist narrativity, that is, certain configurations of the feminine and the masculine in the representation of empirical positivities.

INTRODUCTION
Writing Technologies of the Subject—
From Narrative to Narrativity

> A "domain" is opened in which the inscription, as it is said, of a subject in his text, (so many notions to be reelaborated), is also the condition for the pertinence and performance of a text, of what the text "is worth" beyond what is called an empirical subjectivity, supposing that such a thing exists as soon as it speaks, writes, and substitutes one object for another, substitutes and adds itself as an object to another, in a word, as soon as it *supplements*. The notion of truth is quite incapable of accounting for this performance. (Derrida 1987, p. 322)

Sociologist Richard Harvey Brown (1987) has recently argued that narrative, long in decline, is now "almost dead" (p. 143). Brown draws on Walter Benjamin's (1968, pp. 83-100) argument, in which the decline of the narrative basis of knowledge is described in terms of a displacement of "storytelling" from "the realms of living speech" to the realm of technologically produced mass culture, a loss to narrative of the power and authority of the storyteller. Not only is the mass-produced novel blamed for undermining the construction of a coherent reality in terms of what Benjamin describes as the "natural" relationship of storytelling and historicity, but it is easy to imagine, as Brown seemingly does, that the decline of the narrative basis of knowledge has only become more intense with the development of mass media communication technologies such as film, video, and computerization.

Thus Brown's concern with the decline of narrative is brought to bear on his criticism of a "technicist way of thought," especially as it informs sociological discourse. The trouble with sociology, Brown's argument implies, is that it marginalizes those interpretive methods that are more congenial to narrative and that usually rely on ethnography and participant observation. The statistical methodology that sociological discourse instead privileges supports "banal culture" by equating "the public sphere" with "mass behavior that can be aggregated into statistical facts" (p. 189). Ethnography and participant observation are not only put in opposition to statistical methodology, an often-rehearsed argument in sociology, but it would seem that ethnography and participant observation are understood to be relatively immune to the undermining effects of mass media communication technologies in terms of the narrative basis of knowledge.

This book puts forth a different understanding of the relationships among sociological discourse, narrative, ethnography, and mass media communication technologies. I will argue not only that all factual representations of empirical reality, even statistical representations, are narratively constructed, but that the narrative construction of factuality or empirical positivities has been the dominant form of mass media communication technologies developed since the rise of the realist novel. Furthermore, I will argue not only that the ethnographic form exemplifies the narrative construction of factual representations of empirical reality, but that its narrative strategies are those of the mass media. Therefore, while ethnography is a marginal sociological methodology, it is central to sociological discourse: The ethnography enacts for sociological discourse the authority of the storyteller, in the figure of the heroic ethnographer or participant observer, while adjusting this figure to the various mass media communication technologies. Ethnography is the productive icon of empirical scientific authority.

Of course, at the time of Brown's publication, ethnography and the method of participant observation had already become objects of cultural criticism. In anthropology, "the literarization of the ethnographic text," as Paul Smith (1989) describes it, had already opened up ethnography to a critical analysis of its textual practices. Rather than expressing a concern for the decline of narrative, these criticisms of ethnography underscored the political implications of the narrative production of ethnography's posture as "a general knowledge" that "presignifies or preconceives a totality, a whole, which in function correlates to the subject's own desired wholeness" (Smith 1989, p. 162). Faced, as James Clifford (1988) puts it, "with the breakup and redistribution of colonial power" and with the impossibility of "the West" presenting itself "as the unique purveyor of anthropological knowledge about others" (p. 22), the ethnography became profoundly problematized for the way its ethnocentrism functions in a defensive, imaginary construction of a desired unity in the figure of the ethnographer as the authorized subject of a complete or empirically adequate knowledge.

While these criticisms pointed to the interrelatedness of ethnographic authority and narrative form, they did not further explicate the relationship in narrative of desire and authority. What was not made clear is how the desire that narrative puts into play is nonetheless disavowed so that the unity of the subject and the completeness of knowledge might appear as factual representations of empirical reality rather than the imaginary constructs they were now criticized to be. It was not shown how narrative desire is itself narratively disavowed. I want to propose that it is the realist narrative that informs ethnography that produces the narrative effects of a disavowed desire. It is realist narrativity that makes narrative appear as if nearly dead, dead to desire.

However, understanding both the play and disavowal of desire in the realist narrative requires a shift in the study of narrative to a poststructural, semiotic approach that emphasizes narrative's productivity, that is, how narrative works in the production of meaning. This shift in approach focuses critical attention on what Teresa De Lauretis (1984) describes as "narrativity" or "the transformative effect" of narrative desire produced in and for the subject in the processes of reading and writing (p. 105). Reviewing studies of narratology, De Lauretis argues that the concern of these studies with the function of narrative figures or "dramatis personae," as well as with linearity or the relationship of beginning, middle, and end in modern narrative especially, suggests that *narrativity* refers to the movement in the time/space of the plot, which is also a movement of unconscious desire.

Thus the shift to the study of narrativity also draws on psychoanalysis, not only because of the relationship of narrative and desire, but because desire is disavowed in narrative, shaping the subject of reading and writing unconsciously. It is for this reason that a poststructural, semiotic approach refers to the subject of reading and writing as an effect of narrative desire, thereby reiterating the psychoanalytic understanding that the subject is constructed in unconscious desire. It is also for its understanding of narrative desire that a poststructural, semiotic approach describes the logic of narrativity as an oedipal one.

Thus the psychoanalytic orientation of a poststructural, semiotic approach can be described to return the study of narrativity to Freud's Oedipus, to the relationship of unconscious desire, subject identity, and discursive authority. Briefly put, this relationship refers to Freud's description of the resolution of the Oedipus complex as finally fixing the subject's identity in relationship to his or her parents' desire and in terms of sexual difference—masculinity or femininity. That is, Oedipus elicits the child's sexual identification as a response to what Jacques Lacan (1977) calls "the law of the father," or "the law of the phallus," by which the child is commanded to relinquish the mother as the object of desire. But since, as Freud proposes, the Oedipus complex is never completely or successfully resolved, it is this failure that makes possible various unconscious, fantasmatic, or imaginary (sexual) identifications, even as the possibility of these identifications can also involve their disavowal or denial. Sexual identity is always informed with the loss of the mother as well as the refusal of that loss.

Therefore, while the failure of Oedipus results in unconscious desire for which a unified or fixed sexual identity never coheres, unconscious desire can also inform defensive fantasies in which a coherence of identity is imagined in order to disavow and supplement the failure of identity. Central to these defensive fantasies of a unified sexual identity is the denial of the loss of the mother and all the losses prior to Oedipus that the mother now comes to figure, such as the infant's separation from the womb and the loss of part-objects taken by the infant as parts of him- or herself—the breast, for example. These defensive fantasies thereby figure the subject as appropriating the phallus or the phallic function in distributing the law of difference. The identification usually also involves the refiguring of the loss of the mother as the mother's loss, or "her" castration.

Thus the unconscious defense against a failed sexual identity is fantasmatically constructed by disavowing sexual difference, that is, by reducing sexual difference to a crude anatomical opposition that admits only the phallus (or castration). This is not to say that sexual difference is anatomical difference, as psychoanalysis is so often read to be arguing. Rather, psychoanalysis proposes that it is only in fantasy that sexual difference can be defensively reduced to a crude anatomical opposition in the construction of a unified identity. As Jacqueline Rose (1988) puts it:

> Anatomical difference comes to *figure* sexual difference, that is, it becomes the sole representative of what that difference is allowed to be. It thus covers over the complexity of the child's early sexual life with a crude opposition in which that very complexity is refused or repressed. The phallus thus indicates the reduction of difference to an instance of visible perception, a *seeming* value. (p. 66)

Thus a poststructural, semiotic approach to narrativity draws on psychoanalysis to understand narrative desire and its disavowal in the fantasmatic construction of a unified identity as the authorized subject (of reading and writing). If, as Rose suggests, it is the subject who reduces sexual difference to a crude anatomical opposition in the fantasmatic appropriation of the phallus, then it is the projection and displacement of the subject's oedipal fantasies that poststructural criticism proposes narrativity elicits in reading and writing.

But if a poststructural, semiotic approach to narrativity makes use of psychoanalysis, it is because what psychoanalysis came to describe as the relationship of subject identity, unconscious desire, and sexual difference had already come to inform narrativity in various other discourses of the eighteenth and nineteenth centuries. Narrativity, therefore, refers not only to the subject's unconscious complicity in the processes of reading and writing, but also to institutionalized forms of author(ity), by which the reader and writer are subjugated to and in dominant discourses. As Kaja Silverman (1988) suggests, narrativity functions in the "dominant discourses which make up the larger symbolic order . . . to define and localize the phallus by 'imaging' or 'fantasizing' a speaking subject—a subject authorized to command that discourse's power/ knowledge" (p. 30). Thus arguing that narrativity is informed with an oedipal logic not only implies that narrativity puts unconscious desire into play, drawing on the reader's and writer's losses and failed sexual identities, but also that narrativity can restrict the play of unconscious desire by finally reducing sexual difference to a crude anatomical opposition that disavows loss and sexual difference and that thereby can figure a unified subject identity as author(ity).

If, then, a poststructural, semiotic criticism makes use of psychoanalysis in an analysis of narrative authority, feminist critics of narrative employ psychoanalysis to emphasize the sexual politics by which discursive authority is narratively constructed in the masculine figure, as the divisions of a failed sexual identity are fantasmatically disavowed by displacing them onto the feminine figure of narrative (Penley 1989;

De Lauretis 1984; Rose 1988; Silverman 1988). Thus both poststructural and feminist criticisms of discursive authority propose focusing on an oedipal logic of narrativity in the construction of an archaeology of technologies for the mass public(iz)ation of scenarios of desire that figure a unity of identity in the masculine figure.

In Chapter 1, I will argue that it is an oedipal logic that informs the traditional ethnography, and that this logic is first developed as a narrative logic of mass media throughout the eighteenth century, culminating in the realist novel. Furthermore, while an oedipal logic already informed representations of the subject, at least since Shakespeare's sonnets (Fineman 1986), it is only with the rise of realism that an oedipal logic of narrativity is operated to construct a unified masculine subject identity as the author(ity) of factual representations of empirical reality. Thus, by means of a narrative logic that permits displacements and projections of a disavowed oedipal desire, realist narrativity provides a form for the authorization of readers and writers of factuality or empirical positivities.

Although realist narrativity characterizes both the ethnography and the novel, the two are nonetheless usually taken to be of opposed discourses. In Chapter 1, I will also argue that it is with the rise of realism that fictional and factual discourses become increasingly opposed, even while in the realist narrative itself fact and fiction are actually adjusted to each other, are regulated in relationship to each other as content and form, story and discourse. Indeed, realism is a fantasmatic or unconscious construction of "empirical reality," thereby producing relays between the opposed registers of factual and fictional discourses while nonetheless maintaining their apparent opposition. That is, by producing these relays in terms of the subject's unconscious desire, realist narrativity defends empiricism and factuality from the becoming visible of their narrative constructions, from the becoming visible of writing and reading as desiring productions. Thus realist narrativity always threatens to expose what it means to erase, that is, the fantasmatic construction of the real, of authority, and of the opposition of factual and fictional discourses. Often, realist narrativity stages these threats in the feminine figure so that the masculine figure becomes author by gaining mastery over them by mastering her, containing her threat in narrative closure.

In suggesting that the traditional ethnography shares with the realist novel an oedipal logic of narrativity, I also mean to suggest that sociological discourse and mass media communication technologies, while remaining opposed registers, are nonetheless adjusted to each other through ethnography. That is to say, ethnography functions to provide sociological discourse with realisms shaped in the development of mass media communication technologies. Indeed, I would argue that the realist narrative exists only in the material specificity of its technological inscription, so that narrative, as Mary Ann Doane (1988) has said, "is subject to a thinking inflected by a technological reconstructing of space and time" (p. 80). What I take Doane's remark to suggest, and what I will be arguing throughout this book, is that not only is the realist narrative constrained by a specific mass media communication technology—such as print, film, video, or computer technology—but each technology has been constrained by its capture, so to speak, within realist narrativity. With each technological development, I would propose, the oedipal logic is made again to serve in the deployment of realism and the holding of narrative to the production of factuality and empirical positivities.

Thus the historically specific conjoining of realist narrativity and a mass media technology, resulting, for example, in the novel, classical narrative cinema, the soap-operatic form of television, and computerized simulation, each time involved reconfiguring a unified subject identity in relation to newly regulated relays of fact and fiction in the authorization of representations of empirical reality. I will therefore refer to realist narrativity as it was inscribed in the novel, cinema, television, and computerized simulation as *writing technologies of the subject*. The notion of writing technologies of the subject is a critical one. It is meant to make writing or writing apparatuses more visible; it is meant to make more noticeable the near indistinguishability of the techniques of narrative and the mechanics of mass media communication technologies.

Therefore, I am proposing a view of technology along the lines suggested by Stanley Aronowitz (1988) when he treats technology as a "type of rationality," "a field of perception" (p. 343). Aronowitz argues:

> The mass communication media, perhaps the most powerful technological achievement of this century, are neither extensions of collective human powers, nor an awesome otherness standing against us, but occupy the space of social life such that no relations—those within the psychic structure, or between individuals, or among and between collectivities—can escape the enframing of technology. . . . Technology is not an episteme alone, although it is surely entwined with all forms of knowledge, including language and art; it is the discourse that modifies, when it does not entirely shape, objects as well as the rules of knowledge formation. . . . More to the point, technology as discourse defines social construction. (pp. 343-344)

If, then, various "mass communication media" have enframed configurations of the subject (psychic structure), have regulated what will be constituted for that subject as reality (objects of knowledge), and have established the distribution of persons, places, events, and perspectives in relations of knowledge production (rules of knowledge formation), these effects have been produced through adjustments between realist narrativity and mass media communication technologies. These adjustments, I would argue, serve to maintain empirical science's hegemony. Thus science, nearly identical with writing technologies of the subject, is, as Bruno Latour (1983) describes it, a site for the production of knowledge/power, aligning itself with political, economic arrangements, or what Aronowitz (1988) refers to as "the capital/state axis" (p. 300).

Not that a political, economic arrangement can be made distinct as cause or effect of a particular writing technology of the subject. Rather, a writing technology of the subject can be said to embed within it a certain political, economic arrangement, as part of the labyrinth of texts or social constructs the technology enframes and in terms of which any text or social construct becomes legible. Therefore, the change from one writing technology to another can be made visible only retrospectively as the function of a text or social construct.

In the chapters following, I will reread certain texts as having thematized as their content the formal transference from one writing technology of the subject to another in terms of political, economic arrangements that are at the same time adjustments of realist narrativity and mass media communication technologies. In Chapters 2, 4, and 6, I will offer rereadings of the sociological writings of Herbert Blumer, Howard S. Becker, and Erving Goffman, respectively. I take their writings to constitute a discourse on ethnography, in which the ethnographic method of participant observation is readjusted in terms of writing technologies of the subject. In each of these chapters, I will draw on critical studies of cinema, television, and computer simulation in order to give some sense of realist narrativity as it is inscribed in these technologies; I will then argue that the writings of Blumer, Becker, and Goffman, respectively, inform sociological discourse with a cinematic realism, an emotional realism (of television), and a commercial realism (of computerized simulation).

Each man's writing effects different relays between fact and fiction for the narrative construction of authorized factual representations of empirical reality. Each man's writing increasingly makes narrative desire more visible, so that the unified subject identity of narrative is brought closer to its deconstruction while the function of narrative in the construction of authorized representations of reality is all but acknowledged. However, while these writings bring traditional ethnography closer to the critical reading of it that I offer in Chapter 1, no one of these men's writings, not even all of them together, constitute a poststructural, semiotic approach to ethnography, revealing its function for sociological discourse as a whole. Each writer maintains some semblance of the traditional posture of the heroic ethnographer, refusing a critical analysis of the oedipal logic of realist narrativity. These writers, rather, make uncritical use of an oedipally organized logic of sexual difference to reconstitute empiricism for sociological discourse in terms of various writing technologies of the subject: Blumer in his disavowed eroticization of participant observation, Becker in his redressing social scientific writing by seemingly undressing the sociological writer, and Goffman in his uncovering only for commercial advertisement the oedipal organization of a logic of sexual difference that nonetheless haunts his failed attempts to equate sociology with programming (in)sanity.

If, then, it might be suggested that Goffman's writings bring ethnography to a certain end, it is because in his writing it becomes clearer that the ends of ethnography have been to lend narrative authority to the factual representation of empirical positivities. That is, ethnography provides sociological discourse with a realist narrativity that elicits certain scenarios of unconscious desire in order to disavow the productivity of the unconscious altogether. Goffman's writings all but deconstruct the opposition of factual and fictional discourses, making narrativity more visible not only in the construction of sociological discourse but also in lived experience itself. Goffman's writings provide a sense in which institutionalized discursive arrangements of person, places, events, and perspectives are narratively constructed to constitute lived experience rather than represent it.

If, then, I would argue that the discourse on ethnography has provided social science with various forms of realism in relation to various mass media communication technologies, I would also propose that mass media productions similarly function in the public(iz)ation of new forms of realism. In Chapters 3 and 5, I therefore offer rereadings of various contemporary films—*Alien, Gorillas in the Mist,* and several of Steven Spielberg's productions—in order to suggest that these films function to subvert one writing technology of the subject while giving shape to another. These rereadings are not meant to suggest that these films are ethnographies or that film criticism should replace an ethnography now in decline, but rather that mass media productions also function as the discourse on ethnography does, to readjust realism and mass media communication technologies through an oedipal logic of narrativity, thereby maintaining the ideological hegemony of empiricism in relationship to changing mass media communication technologies. These films are offered as examples of the work that is done by mass media productions to defend the authority of empirical science against the becoming visible of the fantasmatic construction of empirical positivities.

Therefore, I will argue that these films construct as their content oedipal fantasies to disavow Oedipus. Such fantasies function to construct the subject of a new writing technology while proposing new relays between fact and fiction, fantasy and reality, in response to new mass media communication technologies. I have focused my rereadings on the way the change from one writing technology of the subject to another is narratively organized to maintain empiricism's ideological hegemony through reconfiguring the masculine and the feminine in the construction of an authorizing subject identity.

Focusing on the disintegration of the family, the reconstruction of sexualities, and the reworking of gender relationships, the films that I consider not only take oedipal fantasies as their content, they risk revealing that the content of realist representation is no more real than an oedipal fantasy can sustain. In this sense, the focus of these films on issues or events of family, sexuality, and gender is at the same time a display, a deployment of relations of power/knowledge that maintains empiricism as the privileged horizon of reading and writing generally. All in all, then, I would propose a complicity between sociological discourse and mass media in the production of the ideological hegemony of empiricism. This complicity now confronts sociologists as well as critics of culture, literature, film, television, and computerized simulation, thereby urging a poststructural, semiotic approach to discursive authority in general, an approach that needs be informed with both feminist and psychoanalytic orientations.

FEMINISM AND THE DECONSTRUCTION OF ETHNOGRAPHIC REALISMS

Of course, some feminists have already made a psychoanalytic orientation central to rereading cultural productions. Psychoanalysis offered these feminists a way to problematize profoundly the various connotations usually ascribed to the woman as "her nature." Psychoanalysis provided a way to understand these connotations as displacements in the service of a fantasmatic production of a unified subject identity, usually in the masculine figure. But psychoanalysis also proposed that any unified subject identity, even a feminine or feminist identity, is a fantasmatic construction, a construction of unconscious desire. For some feminists, then, not only are all subjectivities divided in unconscious desire, but the divisions of the unconscious are not merely reducible to the divisions and fractures of social, political, economic arrangements.

Perhaps it is this insistence on the persistence of the divisions of the unconscious that has led other feminists, usually social scientists, to resist the poststructural, semiotic approach to criticism and to insist instead on a feminist empirical science (Hartsock 1985; Harding 1986; Haraway 1988; Marcia-Lees, Sharpe, and Cohen 1989). These feminists complain that a psychoanalytic orientation to criticism cannot reconstitute the woman as a unified subject, which, it is argued, is necessary for political action. Thus feminist social scientists, if they allow the unconscious at all, insist on reducing it to experience—that is, to the social, political, economic matrix in which relationships of gender, race, class, ethnicity, and nationality are both constituting and constituted (for a review of this debate, see Penley 1989; Rose 1988).

While feminist social scientists often argue against the unconscious in order to issue theoretically a unified feminist subject that would underwrite political action, a psychoanalytically oriented criticism does not deny political action. It only puts into question a theorized unified feminist subject, the indifference to difference in a unified feminist politics. As Constance Penley (1989) argues:

> If we have learned from psychoanalysis to question the presumed unity of any given subjectivity, why should we feel obliged to drop this critique when it comes to the question of social configurations? "Conscious daily life" is hardly immune to the operations of the unconscious. . . . The task therefore is not to seek the sameness that can unite women as women but to see how that unity can be forged and alliances created, while always staying alert to the (fantasmatic) bases on which they are being made. (p. xviii)

But what Penley fails to recognize, and what I want to emphasize, is that it is the function of sociological discourse to present the empirical positivities of daily life precisely as if everyday experience were immune to the operations of the unconscious.

Not only does sociological discourse disavow the working of unconscious desire in the narrative production of its authority, it also disavows the operations of the unconscious in the daily life it purports to represent. It is for this reason that feminist cultural criticism must be rearticulated as a criticism of the ethnographic realisms of sociological discourse. Feminist social scientists can thus be urged to recognize that realist accounts, whether they be of race, class, ethnicity, gender, or nationality, put into play unconscious fantasy. These accounts not only present the "facts," but, in doing so, they publicize fantasies that authorize the facts as a reality and at the same time authorize empiricism as the horizon of reading and writing generally.

The psychoanalytic orientation of a poststructural, semiotic approach to narrativity is not a proposal for a feminist or cultural criticism that is indifferent to the differences of race, class, gender, ethnicity, and nationality. Nor is it a proposal for an uncritical use of psychoanalysis. What is proposed is a criticism that calls attention to the way realist narrativity makes use of an oedipal logic to reduce differences to a crude opposition, figured as masculine and feminine, and how the terms thus figured are hierarchalized, privileging one term over another. Criticism is focused on the way a logic of sexual difference is made to fantasmatically obtain social, political, and economic oppositions by which the discursive privileging of one term of the opposition over the other appears natural.

Thus a poststructural, semiotic approach also disconnects psychoanalysis from its own investment in realism, from its own pretension to being an empirical science, that is, from its own use of an oedipal logic of narrativity to "naturalize" what it, itself, shows are fantasmatically constructed oppositions. The psychoanalytic orientation of a poststructural, semiotic approach is understood, therefore, only to provide a logic for reconstructing fantasmatic constructions of experience. In such a criticism, representation is referred to what Barbara Johnson (1977) describes as "a *knot* in a structure where words, things and organs can neither be definably separated nor compatibly combined" (p. 498). Criticism, then, is not an "interpretation or an insight but an act. An act of *untying* the knot in the structure by means of the repetitions of the act of tying it" (p. 498).

Therefore, my criticism of ethnographic realisms is not meant to propose a nonnarrative writing, nor is it meant to deny oedipal or unconscious desire; rather, it is intended to focus critical attention on the way narrative makes an oedipal logic serve realism in disavowing unconscious desire in the construction of factual representations of empirical

reality—the way realist narrativity conflates authorized knowledge with a
fantasy of a unified subject identity, masculine or feminine. In Chapter
7, I offer a rereading of Toni Morrison's writings that suggests they
develop a criticism of realist narrativity and its oedipal logic, which figures
the author as masculine. They also struggle with and against figuring
the woman as a unified subject of authority. Not only do Morrison's
writings focus on women's search for identity, but, because the women
of her texts must also labor against the effects of racism, the struggle
for identity is complicated by the desire to correct history, to correct already authorized representations of empirical reality, that is, the desire
to author(ize) another reality.

What is remarkable about Morrison's writings is that a woman's
struggle for identity and her desire to authorize another reality are not
allowed to collapse into one another. That is, realist narrativity is not
allowed to appropriate an oedipal logic for the construction of a unified
subject identity. Nor are loss and sexual difference disavowed, at least
not finally in Morrison's most recent work, *Beloved*. Thus, while a
woman's claim to authority involves her in an appropriation of the phallic function and the disavowal of sexual difference, a woman's search
for identity would seemingly make necessary a rearticulation of sexual
difference that is not a crude reduction to an anatomical opposition.
Morrison's writings work on this contradiction; they act out and act
upon an oedipal logic of realist narrativity.

While the question of the relationship of narrativity, identity, and
authority is raised in Morrison's first book, *The Bluest Eye*, in *Sula*
identity and authority are conflated in the interest of constructing a
unified feminine subject identity. I reread *Sula* to be informed with an
oedipal fantasy to disavow Oedipus, loss, and sexual difference. This
fantasmatic disavowal enables the woman writer by seemingly return-
ing her to the pre-oedipal space of mother and infant before Oedipus re-
orders the separation of mother and infant in terms of sexual difference.
But if in *Sula* the exclusive relationship of woman to woman enables a
woman's writing, that writing ends in a silence that in *Beloved* speaks
a bitterness and resentment that consume the mother and daughter in
their exclusivity. In *Beloved,* the fantasmatic denial of Oedipus is
worked through and the woman's search for identity ends in a subjectivity, indefinitely divided in desire. Thus, without denying Oedipus,
Morrison deconstructs the oedipal logic of realist narrativity, making
writing visible as a desiring production, a fantasy to make the impos-
sible a fictional possibility for living.

My rereading of Toni Morrison's writings is meant to propose a narrativity that neither denies unconscious desire nor merely reproduces the oedipal logic of realist narrativity in the deployment of relations of knowledge/power. While Morrison's writings are conducive to political understanding and to the affirmation of women's interests—in particular, African-American women's interests—they do so not as an analysis of empirical reality, but as an exploration of desire. In a particular way, they model a feminist reading and writing beyond the realisms that I will consider throughout this book. Morrison's writings suggest a way for sociological discourse to reconstitute itself as social criticism.

REFERENCES

Aronowitz, Stanley. 1988. *Science as Power.* Minneapolis: University of Minnesota Press.

Benjamin, Walter. 1968. *Illuminations.* New York: Harcourt Brace.

Brown, Richard Harvey. 1987. *Society as Text.* Chicago: University of Chicago Press.

Clifford, James. 1988. *The Predicament of Culture.* Cambridge, MA: Harvard University Press.

De Lauretis, Teresa. 1984. *Alice Doesn't: Feminism, Semiotics, Cinema.* Bloomington: Indiana University Press.

Derrida, Jacques. 1987. *The Post Card.* Translated by A. Bass. Chicago: University of Chicago Press.

Doane, Mary Ann. 1988. "The Abstraction of a Lady: *La Signore di tutti.*" *Cinema Journal* 28(Fall): 65-84.

Fineman, Joel. 1986. *Shakespeare's Perjured Eye: The Invention of Poetic Subjectivity in the Sonnets.* Berkeley: University of California Press.

Haraway, Donna. 1988. "Situated Knowledges: The Science Question in Feminism and the Privilege of Partial Perspectives." *Feminist Studies* 14(Fall): 575-599.

Harding, Sandra. 1986. *The Science Question in Feminism.* Ithaca, NY: Cornell University Press.

Hartsock, Nancy. 1985. *Money, Sex and Power.* Boston: Northeastern University Press.

Johnson, Barbara. 1977. "The Frame of Reference: Poe, Lacan and Derrida." *Yale French Studies* 55/57: 457-505.

Lacan, Jacques. 1977. *Ecrits.* Translated by Alan Sheridan. New York: W. W. Norton.

Latour, Bruno. 1983. "Give Me a Laboratory." In *Science Observed,* edited by K. D. Knorr-Cetina and M. Mulkay. London: Sage.

Marcia-Lees, Frances, Patricia Sharpe, and Colleen Ballerino Cohen. 1989. "The Postmodernist Turn in Anthropology: Cautions from a Feminist Perspective." *Signs* 15: 7-33.

Penley, Constance. 1989. *The Future of an Illusion: Film, Feminism, and Psychoanalysis.* Minneapolis: University of Minnesota Press.

Rose, Jacqueline. 1988. *Sexuality in the Field of Vision.* London: Verso.

Silverman, Kaja. 1988. *The Acoustic Mirror: The Female Voice in Psychoanalysis and Cinema.* Bloomington: Indiana University Press.

Smith, Paul. 1989. "Writing, General Knowledge, and Postmodern Anthropology." *Discourse* 11.2(Spring-Summer): 159-170.

1

ETHNOGRAPHIC AUTHORITY AND
THE OEDIPAL LOGIC
OF REALIST NARRATIVITY

The work of narrative, then, is a mapping of differences, and specifically, first and foremost, of sexual difference into each text; and hence, by a sort of accumulation, into the universe of meaning, fiction, and history, represented by the literary-artistic tradition and all the texts of culture. (De Lauretis 1984, p. 121)

James Clifford (1983) begins his now well-known essay on "ethnographic authority" by contrasting the frontispiece of Father Lafitau's 1724 *Moeurs des Sauvages Ameriquains* with the frontispiece of Bronislaw Malinowski's 1922 *Argonauts of the Western Pacific.* The latter, a photograph of a Trobriand chief during a ceremonial act, signifies for Clifford the way in which this ethnography is "archetypical of the generation of ethnographies that successfully established participant-observation's scientific validity" (pp. 123-124). The anthropologist is not to be seen, but his presence is felt in the gaze of the camera that holds forth to view the captured "reality of the other." "The predominant mode of modern field work authority is signaled: 'You are there, because I was there' " (p. 118).

Father Lafitau's frontispiece shows a winged figure of Father Time pointing to a vision just above him of Adam and Eve. At a writing table, facing the figure of Father Time, is, as Lafitau puts it, "a person in the posture of one writing" (quoted in de Certeau 1980: 39). Clifford merely notes that the person is a woman, but de Certeau argues that the figure of the woman is central to understanding this engraving as a presentation of ethnography in relationship to writing and the discourse of empirical science.

Putting the writer on the stage replaces sixteenth and seventeenth-century engravings' representations of meetings between Europeans and Savages, and makes a star out of a new hero of history: the power of writing. In the text itself, the author always marks his place; he underlines what caused him "pain" or gave him "pleasure"; he specifies his intentions, his methods or his successes. These notations make of the writer, or of his written production, an important, if not essential, actor in the "narration." (pp. 50-51)

Rereading Lafitau's frontispiece as one version of an oedipally organized logic of sexual difference, de Certeau argues that the many artifacts scattered around the room in which the woman writes (Astarte, the Isis Mammosa, the Diana of Ephesis) refer to mothering and thus situate the woman writer as a maternal figure, a genitrix (p. 50). The woman, de Certeau concludes, figures the male's desire to engender the powerful writing of empirical science; she figures his desire to make the new writing technology his. But then, to present the male writer in the guise of a woman just when writing is becoming an institutional power in relationship to empirical science is to figure the male writer's subjugation to the power of the new writing technology, even as he breaks with the authority of an "older" tradition of writing. That is, displacing castration onto the woman as her "natural" defect, the male writer is not only able to identify with her, posturing himself as a humble and passive recipient of a writing technology that is powerful in itself. He is also able finally to distinguish himself from her, claiming his own authority in surpassing the authority of an older tradition of writing. The figure of the woman mediates the transformation of power and authority; she becomes more generally the figurative ground on which the writer establishes himself as author in relationship to a powerful writing.

Indeed, de Certeau (1980) argues that the writer of ethnography first appears in the guise of the woman because ethnography is initially in competition with an "older" form of writing, that is, the contemplation and transcription of biblical revelation (p. 53). Ethnography instead proposes a writing that seemingly owes nothing to the contemplation of historical tradition and everything to the observational methodology of empirical scientific research. Ethnography, therefore, founds itself on "a form (a network of formal relations)" that "consists more in what scientific research *gives itself* as work rules than in what it *receives* as a law of history" (p. 53). If, then, in Lafitau's frontispiece, Adam and Eve replace Moses, as de Certeau argues they do, it is to put in place of a historical character the figures of an originary fiction, in which terms the figure of the woman writer is also articulated. Lafitau's frontispiece suggests that Adam and Eve provide the narrative or fictional origin upon which the formal relations of empirical science must necessarily be propped and in terms of which the writer presents himself as author(ity).

If, then, the figure of the woman is first put to use in the fictional or narrative construction of the masculine subject as the author(ity) of ethnography, in what follows I want to argue that as an established writing technology, the traditional ethnography is informed with a fictional or narrative logic that continues to employ the feminine figure in the construction of ethnography's author(ity). I also want to suggest that the narrative logic of ethnography is the oedipal logic of realist narrativity, which established itself during the eighteenth and nineteenth centuries as the generic form of all factual representations of empirical reality.

OEDIPAL LOGIC, NARRATIVITY, AND WRITING ETHNOGRAPHY

If Lafitau's frontispiece suggests that an empirical scientific methodology leans on a narrative or fictional construction, Malinowski's frontispiece suggests what events that narrative would typically dramatize in the name of empiricism: the trials of the researcher in the field. In entering the field, the discipline and dispassion of the ethnographer's empirical methodology are put on trial; they are shown to be triumphant only when, having suffered the experiences of fieldwork, the researcher is able to leave the field and return home to write.

Staging the researcher's entering and leaving the field, the ethnography demonstrates that a boundary has been twice crossed, making possible the empirical correspondences, comparisons, and contrasts (across that boundary) that the ethnography presents as factual representations of cultural perspectives, historical events, and social situations. In the ethnography, these correspondences, comparisons, and contrasts are authoritatively distributed in terms of a narrative logic that establishes a boundary by figuring the field of research as feminine, that is, as the

site of obstacle and trial for the researcher, who is consequently figured
as masculine hero. Thus the ethnography is informed with a narrative
logic by which the hero and the obstacles are always morphologically
masculine and feminine, regardless of their textual personification. This
logic of sexual difference, which I have described as an oedipal logic,
underwrites the narrative construction of correspondences, contrasts,
and comparisons. As Teresa De Lauretis (1984) puts it:

> Opposite pairs such as inside/outside, the raw/the cooked, or life/death
> appear to be merely derivatives of the fundamental opposition between
> boundary and passage; and if passage may be in either direction, from
> inside to outside or vice versa, from life to death or vice versa, nonetheless
> all these terms are predicated on the *single* figure of the hero who crosses
> the boundary and penetrates the other space. In so doing the hero, the myth-
> ical subject, is constructed as human being and as male; he is the active
> principle of culture, the establisher of distinction, the creator of differences.
> Female is what is not susceptible to transformation, to life or death; she (it)
> is an element of plot-space, a topos, a resistance, matrix and matter. (p. 119)

In the ethnography, however, the ethnographer is not the only subject
of the story. His story stages other stories, those of the subjects of the
research. But their stories are also oedipally organized around their
efforts to realize themselves as subjects of knowledge. They too are
shown in their struggle to master the obstacles to knowledge with which
their social, historical, and cultural situations confront them. The subjectivities, like that of the ethnographer, are effects of a narrative construction that nonetheless finally figures them as the heroic subjects of
their own stories. The ethnography generally constructs a subject who,
in the end, appears to be the establisher of those distinctions by which
he is distinguished, the creator of those differences by which he is differentiated. Therefore, the descriptions of cultural, social, and historical
situations that the ethnography puts forth in the relative terms of empirical
correspondences depend for their authority on the narrative construction of the subject.

In this sense, it can be argued that the ethnographic narrative sustains
the function of the subject in the production of an authorized knowledge
of culture, history, and society. The ethnography is itself an authoritative assignment of what Homi Bhabha (1986) describes as "frames of
reference" with which to act and "frames of mind" with which to know
(p. 170); the ethnography is a distribution of perspectives, persons,
places, and events in relations of power/knowledge. Thus, rather than

the production of partial knowledge specific to the perspective of an individual researcher, ethnography is a production of frames that are partial to empirical science and its allied interests.

While these frames are narrative productions, they are nonetheless authorized in and for a subject; they are nonetheless attributed by the narrative to ethnographic subjectivity, in the figure of the ethnographer/ author. If, then, the ethnographer's trials in the field, which the ethnography dramatizes, finally figure the ethnographer as the heroic subject of knowledge, it makes "personal" only what the narrative itself constructs as ethnographic authority. This personalization, however, is central to ethnography, since the textual production of cultural, historical, and social knowledge is dependent on what Bryan Green (1988) describes as the "projection of an integral identity ahead of words and actions so that the latter are encountered as indexical expressions of the former" (p. 33). A practice of reading and writing, productive of cultural, historical, and social knowledge, depends on a subject identity that shapes knowledge as a "personal" and therefore "integral vision of social life" (p. 34). But Green, following Harold Bloom (1973), emphasizes that the subject identity that underwrites knowledge is a formal construction, found in a text as "a semiotic structure emerging from defensive transformations of an immanent, intrinsic, threatening pressure" (Green 1988, p. 68). This pressure in terms of which identity forms arises as the writer's oedipal struggle with a precursor writer or writing —the struggle, that is, to appropriate the phallic function of writing itself (p. 69).

It might be argued, then, that in the case of the ethnography, the display of the ethnographer's struggles as well as those of the subjects of his research appear at the surface of the text only as the manifest or screened content of another struggle, the struggle of authorial desire. This struggle is always at another scene than that of the field research— the scene of reading and writing. Thus, while the ethnography impresses authorial desire in the textual surface of the content of empirical science, it nevertheless disavows desire in that the content is a defensive transformation of desire that makes it appear as nothing but factual representations of empirical reality. In what follows, I therefore want to argue that it is the realist narrative as it developed during the eighteenth and nineteenth centuries that informs ethnography with a narrative authority that always refers factual representation to the other scene of reading and writing.

THE REALIST NARRATIVE:
THE CONTENT OF FORM

Michael McKeon (1987), in his study of the rise of the realist novel, argues that the novel is first recognized as a distinct genre when what develops as two distinct questions come to be understood or answerable with a single response, that is, when the realist novel successfully demonstrates that these two questions are "more tractable when seen as analogous versions of each other" (p. 22). The first of these questions concerned the "truth of representation" and was put forth in response to empiricism and its demand for historicity, or the completeness and adequacy of evidence. The second question concerned the integrity or unity of a subject identity in terms of self-development. This question arose in response to the shift from feudalism to capitalism, with the decline of the aristocracy and the rise of the self-made, self-authored man.

McKeon notes that in the debates around these two questions, the opponents of one response referred to the other responses, which they rejected, as romantic or fiction. Thus empiricism first presented itself as a critique of romance or fiction, in its proposing instead "an optimistic ambition to construct the positive laws of universal history" (p. 4). But this version of empiricism provoked a countercritique that viewed this first version as itself romantic, naive, or fictional. This countercritique, "extreme skepticism," presented itself as a more chastened empiricism. It held that "every historical period is singular and perhaps unknowable from without" (p. 41), but that understanding experience in its historical specificity allows for a factuality in the general relevance of "the truth of things."

The debates around an integrity or unity of identity were similarly structured. Thus, in resistance to the "aristocratic ideology" of lineage and inheritance, a "progressive ideology" positively emphasized the self-production of a truly integrated character. But in response to progressive ideology, "conservative ideology," while accepting the constructed nature of identity, nevertheless rejected as fictional "the capitalizing of spirit," which it claimed progressive ideology falsely held as true. It proposed instead "useful fictions of inherited authority," socially useful fictions of the development of the individual's "inherent" character (p. 201).

Thus the contention over truth had become a debate over the value or worth of fact versus fiction, which during the eighteenth century was argued in terms of the completeness or historical adequacy of representation as well as in terms of the integrity or unity of a self-developed subject identity. When these debates were finally resolved in a valorization of realism, it was because the realist novel made it possible to answer both questions in terms of each other by maintaining the opposition of fact and fiction even while constructing relays between these opposed registers in the narrative interaction of discourse and story or form and content. In the realist novel, therefore, a narrative form evolved by which the development of the unity or integrity of a subject identity (whether that be conceived in terms of a progressive or a conservative ideology) became itself the form of the author(ization) of factual representations of empirical reality (whether that be conceived in terms of a naive or skeptical empiricism). In the novel's representing all experience as the experience of a self-development, the final realization of the unity of that development comes to author(ize) those experiences as factual representations of empirical reality. The realist novel thereby formalizes the self-production of a unified subject identity as its discursive or narrative form, as the generic form of all factual representations of empirical reality.

The realist novel, then, formally manages a paradox it puts into play; it meets its own demand for a unified subject identity that author(izes) the story even though the subject identity cannot be realized as an integrated unity until the end of the story, when the subject's self-development has been actualized as a whole. The realist narrative manages this paradox by presenting the story of a character's self-development as a reconstructed history in which the end of the story is always already known at the beginning while the realization of this knowledge is always deferred to the end. Thus the story is narrated by a subject who, while sharing the time-space of the story, possibly as one of the characters or even the main character, is nonetheless distinct from the story. The narrating subjectivity belongs, that is, to the discursive production of the story and is the discursive, fictional, or narrative agency of the story's author(ity).

From the start, then, the narrating subjectivity guarantees both the unity of the character's identity and the completeness or historical adequacy of the story. Whatever the story shows or makes knowable as the character's developmental experiences are therefore retroactively authorized when the story exactly realizes what was discursively prefigured in and projected forward by the narrating subjectivity of the discourse.

But if the narrating subjectivity knows from the start what the story finally realizes, the scenes of the realist narrative are not so much presentations of a temporally unfolding reality as they appear to be. They are more representations, projections of a movement that is always forward to the end(s) of knowledge but at the same time always backward to the narrating subjectivity of the discourse, to the authority governing the story. The reconstructive logic of the realist narrative therefore informs the story with an "inner drive" by which the story's ending is always imagined as a recapturing of the "lost" origin of the subject's desire to know himself, to author himself. That is, the desire of the realist narrative is an oedipal desire with which the past is rewritten and the present is desired to the end(s) of the subject's self-knowledge, his unified self-development.

If, then, what the story shows and makes knowable can be read by any reader as factual representations of empirical reality, it is because the narrating subjectivity of the discourse elicits the reader's unconscious identification with the character of the story. The story of the character's self-development comes to be motivated by the reader's displacements and projections of unconscious desire. But if an identification with the character of the story allows for the productivity of the reader's desire in the construction of empirical reality, it also makes possible the disavowal of the reader's desire because the desire of the character with whom the reader is identified, is both displayed and disavowed. That is, the story is itself about the character's struggle to realize and disavow an (oedipal) desire for authority and recognition.

Indeed, Norman Bryson (1984) suggests that in early realist painting, the struggle for authority and recognition is made visible in scenes composed of a privatized and domestic morality or the psychosexuality of the characters. Thus a desire is often displayed that is disallowed realization. That is, desire is disclosed and denied or disavowed in terms of a paternal interdiction acted out in these scenes seemingly among fathers, mothers, and sons, between masters and their servants, between leaders and their followers. The display of desire is always a disclosure of the character as yet incomplete, fractured and wanting what appears therefore as external to him, as an independent reality that contains what is desired. The experiences of the character's self-development become legible in desire, especially in the impossibilities of desire's fulfillment, implying the castration anxiety that informs the story of development as a reconstructed history of desire and its vicissitudes.

It is not surprising, then, that Bryson also finds an oedipal logic of sexual difference operating in these scenes by which the character's struggle for authority and recognition is figuratively articulated in terms of a crude sexual opposition—the masculine figures the subject of desire and the feminine figures the object desired. By means of this logic, the disclosures of the character as incomplete, fractured, and divided in desire are always erased and disavowed as the masculine figure prefigures the final unity of the subject in his heroic mastering of the feminine object of desire. In figuring the desired object as feminine, the masculine figure is always already indicated as the unified subject of the story—the one who is "naturally" expected to recover the phallic function held in advance by the narrating subjectivity of the discourse. Thus the scenes of the paintings thematize the narrative's oedipal form.

If, then, realist narrativity elicits the reader's unconscious desire by means of sexual difference, it is only finally to disavow desire by the disavowal of sexual difference, thereby erasing the narrative construction of empirical reality and allowing representation to appear as nothing but the sheer facticity of empirical positivities. Since desire is denied by a disavowal of sexual difference in the very narrated scenes that elicit desire, the scenes of realist narrativity are rather screens upon which a disavowed oedipal or authorial desire is displaced or projected. But then the realist narrative inscribes not only the reader's unconscious desire, it must inscribe the writer's unconscious desire as well.

Indeed, in terms of the realist narrativity of painting, Bryson (1984) argues that the oedipal struggle of the characters of the story "articulates with the tropes by which the painter organizes his inheritance" (p. 50). That is, the narrated scenes screen not only the reader's desire but also the desire necessary to the writer's or painter's struggle to become an author by distinguishing himself from an already authorized tradition. As Bryson puts it:

> Separation from tradition occurs only when the painter is brought back to himself or revealed to himself by his desire, since the lack at work in desire draws a line around himself, while at the same time establishing tradition as the background against which his identity emerges. (p. 129)

What uniquely characterizes realism, however, is that the writer's or painter's struggle with an authorial desire is posed specifically in terms of empiricism. The writer breaks with an authorial tradition and establishes his own authority not by displaying his artistry, but by confirming the authenticity of his vision, the originality of his knowledge in terms of the completeness or historical adequacy of the representation. Like the reader's desire, the author's desire must necessarily be disavowed in and by the narrative scenes that evoke it. Realism therefore is not only uniquely characterized by the informing of representation with narrativity, but, as Michael Fried (1980) argues, narrativity came to be required in the realist representation in order to persuade or to insist that nothing about the story was posed or composed—nothing, that is, exists merely for the reader; nothing exists merely because it is narrated (written or painted).

In realism, then, narrativity is given a particular function: It permits characters to be presented as if they are completely absorbed in their own activities and therefore are seemingly completely unaware of the beholder and the painter outside the painting or the reader and writer outside the text. The "supreme fiction," as Fried describes this production of the seeming nonexistence of the reader or the beholder, the writer or the painter, refers to a process of narrative unity or closure by which "to forestall and extinguish" in the story itself any traces of the reader or the writer's awareness (p. 103). The process in realist narrativity of displacing or projecting desire is also a process by which desire is disavowed. Narrativity confines desire in "the realm of the manifest content of the objectively representable"; it only allows desire to surface as the sheer facticity of empirical reality (Fried 1987, p. 67).

Therefore, the oedipal organization in realist narrativity, of a logic of sexual difference, is operated not only to figure authority in the unified masculine subject but also to disavow narrative desire or narrativity itself in the factual representation of empirical reality. Factuality is always composed as a narrative defense against narrativity. This defensiveness is itself denied, Fried suggests, as the "real" is made to "affront" the characters of the story. In representing the characters as horrified by the scene (or aspects of the scene) in which they appear, realist narrativity produces "a new and stupefyingly powerful experience of the 'real' " (p. 64). The real is made to appear over and against the characters, as if threatening with castration and therefore provoking a castration anxiety for the reader and writer. The stories thus become, for the reader and writer, screens for the fantasmatic construction of castration anxiety in relationship to the struggle against an already authorized or phallic tradition as well as in relationship to the struggle to master the external world that contains the object of the desiring character's desire.

Castration anxiety is manifested in the content of realist representation through an oedipally organized logic of sexual difference that allows for two thematizations of castration, which Fried (1987, p. 69) describes as masculine and feminine. The masculine thematization refers to the father and son; it thematizes castration as "regulated, masterly, and in the end healing" (p. 69). The feminine thematization refers to the mother and the son; it thematizes castration as "chaotic, hysterical, and unassuageable" (p. 69). Thus the masculine thematization allows for the rejection of an authoritative or paternal tradition while permitting the establishment of another one. However, since in realism the claim to authority is made in terms of an authenticity of vision—that is, the completeness or historical adequacy of representation—this transfer of paternal authority must also be staged in terms of the masculine subject's struggle with the not yet, if ever, masterable external world. Thus the feminine thematization of castration that registers the male's struggle with the external world defensively covers over the struggle among men over phallic power. The feminine figure "naturalizes" the masculine subject's appropriation of the phallic function; it permits the masculine figure to embody the phallic function, as if naturally. The feminine figure, then, is one that Eve Kosofsky Sedgwick (1985) describes as a "chiasmic figure," because through it the phallic function is passed from one masculine subject to another, without the implied divisions in masculine subjectivity becoming noticeable; the feminine figure makes the whole fantasmatic construction of the subject invisible in narrative by disguising and defusing across its surface the homoerotic pleasure/pain of one masculine subject's over-taking/taking-over another masculine subject.

If, then, the oedipal logic of sexual difference secures the final figure of the unified masculine subject as the author(ity) of a complete or historically adequate representation of empirical reality, this logic also provides the means by which the real is narratively constituted. The realist narrative defines the real by a regulation of difference. That is, differences are reduced to crude oppositions and then, by figuring the opposed terms or registers as masculine and feminine, a hierarchalization is made possible that privileges whatever is figured as masculine. Thus the oedipal logic of realist narrativity is a production of relays and exchanges between oppositions that erases difference. By the seeming naturalness of its reduction of (sexual) difference to a crude (anatomical) opposition, the oedipal logic allows the erasure of difference in the narrative production of the real to remain invisible, that is, unconscious.

It is for this reason that realist narrativity can be said to function ideologically. The relationship between realist narrativity and the rise of the bourgeoisie, a focus of much Marxist criticism (Lukacs 1971; Goldman 1975; Williams 1977; Jameson 1981), is not so much a matter of realism's reflecting a bourgeois life-style or privileging a bourgeois culture. Realist narrativity is ideological for making invisible the relays it produces between terms it opposes. Especially important are the relays it produces between those oppositions upon which bourgeois individualism depends, such as self and society, nature and environment, sexuality and economy, private and public.

Thus, while realism seemingly privileges the self-authored (bourgeois) individual, the relays that the realist narrative produces between self and society, nature and environment, sexuality and economy, private and public permit the individual subject to become legible only in terms of the relays and exchanges between oppositions as these constitute the real—culture, history, or society, as these constitute the (sociological) chances in terms of which the individual struggles to realize a self-identity. Indeed, Mark Seltzer (1987) suggests that realist narrativity is a form in which bourgeois individualism overlaps with what he describes as "statistical personation." Like realist narrativity, statistics make the subject an effect of those regularities of the real against which the individual struggles for self-definition. Thus, while statistics produce "regularities irreducible to individual intentions," they nonetheless "provide models of individualization: models for the generic, typical or average man—what we might describe as the production of individuals as statistical persons" (p. 90). Statistics put into play "an oscillation between autonomy and regulation," just as the realist narrativity of the novel and the ethnography construct a subject as author of the distinctions and differentiations by which he is distinguished and differentiated.

Thus, in its narrative construction of the subject, ethnographic realism functions not so much to suppress the voices of the researcher or the subjects of research, as many criticisms of ethnography would imply (Crapanzano 1977; Dwyer 1977; Clifford and Marcus 1986; Clifford 1988; Woolgar and Ashmore 1988; Trinh 1989; Ashmore 1989), but rather embodies voices as statistical personations, events, situations, and perspectives. This politic of embodiment with which ethnographic realism informs sociological discourse and empirical social science generally permits the authoritative distribution of subjects in relations of power/knowledge. What is suppressed or, better, disavowed is the desire installed in the mechanisms of narrativity that make the fantasmatic construction of a unified subject identity the linchpin of empirical science's appropriation of subjectivities for disciplinary relations and allied political economic arrangements.

If, then, it is to be concluded that ethnography is informed with an oedipal logic of realist narrativity, developed through the eighteenth and early nineteenth centuries, it is because ethnography treats the subject's struggle for self-knowledge as a struggle to obtain factual representations of empirical reality. Thus, these representations of empirical reality always screen an oedipal desire to establish authority against a tradition of writing and reading. By figuring the generic or ordinary individual's struggle for identity, the ethnographer authorizes as empirical reality those experiences that seemingly affront any and every individual in their struggle for identity. The authorized reality that the ethnography produces, then, is an effect of the projections and displacements of unconscious oedipal desire. Thus, through ethnography, factual representations of empirical reality are supplemented with the pleasure/pain of the imaginary, fantasmatic construction of a unified subject identity, an identification with which narrativity both elicits from and offers to the reader and the writer.

It is precisely because these identifications are unconscious that factual representations of empirical reality can function as screens for the projection and displacement of the reader's and writer's desire. It is also through these identifications that the reader and writer "see" what is represented as real to them. In making vision a distribution, a delegation, a substitution in desire, ethnographic realism provides sociological discourse with a capacity or agency for making visible. Thus ethnographic realism provides sociological discourse with a kind of vision that even in the eighteenth century, Fried (1980, p. 143) argues, deserved to be called cinematic. I would argue that it is cinematic realism, developed in narrative cinema, that informs the discourse on participant observation, establishing it as an empirical scientific methodology and as central to ethnographic research and sociological discourse.

REFERENCES

Ashmore, Malcolm. 1989. *The Reflexive Thesis.* Chicago: University of Chicago Press.
Bhabha, Homi. 1986. "Signs Taken for Wonders: Questions of Ambivalence and Authority Under a Tree Outside Delhi, May 1817." In *"Race," Writing, and Difference,* edited by Henry Louis Gates, Jr. Chicago: University of Chicago Press.
Bloom, Harold. 1973. *The Anxiety of Influence.* New York: Oxford University Press.
Bryson, Norman. 1984. *Tradition and Desire from David to Delacroix.* New York: Cambridge University Press.
Clifford, James. 1983. "On Ethnographic Authority." *Representations* 1(Spring): 118-146.
———. 1988. *The Predicament of Culture.* Cambridge: Cambridge University Press.
Clifford, James and George Marcus. 1986. *Writing Culture.* Berkeley: University of California Press.

Crapanzano, Vincent. 1977. "The Writing of Ethnography." *Dialectical Anthropology* 2(1): 69-73.

de Certeau, Michel. 1980. "Writing vs. Time: History and Anthropology in the Works of Lafitau." *Yale French Studies* 59: 37-64.

De Lauretis, Teresa. 1984. *Alice Doesn't: Feminism, Semiotics, Cinema*. Bloomington: Indiana University Press.

Dwyer, Kevin. 1977. "On the Dialogic of Fieldwork." *Dialectical Anthropology* 2(2): 143-151.

Fried, Michael. 1980. *Absorption and Theatricality: Painting and Beholder in the Age of Diderot*. Chicago: University of Chicago Press.

———. 1987. *Realism, Writing, Disfiguration: On Thomas Eakins and Stephen Crane*. Chicago: University of Chicago Press.

Goldman, Lucien. 1975. *Towards a Sociology of the Novel*. London: Tavistock.

Green, Bryan. 1988. *Literary Methods and Sociological Theory*. Chicago: University of Chicago Press.

Jameson, Fredric. 1981. *The Political Unconscious*. Ithaca, NY: Cornell University Press.

Lukacs, Georg. 1971. *The Theory of the Novel*. London: Merlin.

McKeon, Michael. 1987. *The Origins of the English Novel 1600-1740*. Baltimore: Johns Hopkins University Press.

Sedgwick, Eve Kosofsky. 1985. *Between Men: English Literature and Male Homosocial Desire*. New York: Columbia University Press.

Seltzer, Mark. 1987. "Statistical Persons." *Diacritics* 17(Fall): 82-98.

Trinh, Minh-ha. 1989. *Woman, Native, Other*. Bloomington: Indiana University Press.

Williams, Raymond. 1977. *Marxism and Literature*. Oxford: Oxford University Press.

Woolgar, Steve and M. Ashmore. 1988. "The Next Step: Introduction to the Reflexive Project." In *Knowledge and Reflexivity: New Frontiers in the Sociology of Knowledge*, edited by Steve Woolgar. London: Sage.

2

HERBERT BLUMER
A Methodology for Writing Observation

> Blumer always insisted that our theoretical language make room for what everyone could see if they only looked. (Becker 1988, p. 16)

Charles Lemert (1979) has argued that Herbert Blumer's writings on sociological method urge the social scientist to be no more than a "humble listener to a social world which speaks," but nearly all of the remarks with which Lemert represents Blumer's writings are as much about looking as they are about listening. Arguing that Blumer generates the notion of "sensitizing concepts" to provide "tools whereby the scientist listens to the world" (p. 115), Lemert quotes Blumer (1969): "Whereas definitive concepts provide prescriptions of what to see, sensitizing concepts merely suggest directions along which to look" (p. 148).[1] Indeed, Blumer's writings suggest that what the social scientist is to obtain from listening to the world is a way to look at it so as to see it as it really is.

It is with a promise of vision that Blumer recommends the "naturalistic method" of participant observation to all empirical social science, sociology especially. And it is with this promise, I would propose, that the discourse on participant observation methodology comes to inform

Author's Note: An earlier version of this chapter appeared as "The Movies and Social Observation: Reading Blumer's *Movies and Conduct*," in *Symbolic Interaction*, Vol. 11, No. 1, pp. 159-170. Copyright 1988 by JAI Press, Inc. Used by permission of the publisher.

empirical social science with a cinematic realism, developed in narrative cinema in the first half of the twentieth century. Like cinematic realism, the discourse on participant observation methodology makes conceptions of the empirical world dependent on mastering that world through vision. And, like cinematic realism, the discourse on participant observation methodology makes use of an oedipal logic of sexual difference by which that mastery is narratively engendered.

In 1933, Herbert Blumer authored a volume and coauthored a second volume of the Payne Fund study of the movies that focused on the ways cinematic images affect the viewing subject. Although images are also central to Blumer's discussion of participant observation, there is no reference in that discussion to the mass media technology of motion pictures. In what follows, however, I want to reread Blumer's methodological writings in terms of contemporary film criticism, especially feminist film criticism, in order to suggest that Blumer's proposal for participant observation methodology informs empirical social science with strategies of (en)vision(ing) that draw on the reader and writer's familiarity with cinematic codes and imaging. Just as vision is authoritatively constructed in cinema through the figures of narrative, the discourse on participant observation makes the narration of a researcher's struggle for vision essential to the production of the authority of empirical social science. It is this narration, I would propose, that finally underwrites what Blumer describes as the distinction of "scientific conception" from "mere perception."

SCIENTIFIC CONCEPTION
AND PARTICIPANT OBSERVATION

What recommends the naturalistic method of participant observation, as Blumer (1969) describes it, is that it "respects and stays close to the empirical domain" (p. 46). Rather than "pre-set images" becoming "a substitute" for "first hand acquaintance with the sphere of life under study" (p. 37), naturalistic observation permits a "faithful reportorial depiction" of the empirical world (p. 152). But this is not to say that there is no relationship between observing the empirical world and concepts, images, or pictures of that world. Indeed, all of Blumer's prescriptions for the participant observer fold back on the relationship he proposes between conceptions, pictures, or images of the empirical world and the real or obdurate character of that world:

To indicate anything, human beings must see it from their perspective; they must depict it as it appears to them. In this sense no fault can be found with the contention that the empirical world necessarily exists always in the form of human pictures and conceptions of it. However, this does not shift "reality," as so many conclude, from the empirical world to the realm of imagery and conception. One errs if he thinks that since the empirical world can exist for human beings only in terms of images or conceptions of it, therefore reality must be sought in images or conceptions independent of an empirical world. . . . The position is untenable because of the fact that the empirical world can "talk back" to our pictures of it or assertions about it—talk back in the sense of challenging and resisting, or not bending to, our images or conceptions of it. This resistance gives the empirical world an obdurate character that is the mark of reality. The fact that one can accommodate or resolve the resistance only by forming a new image or conception does not free the empirical world of its obdurate character. It is this obdurate character of the empirical world—its ability to resist and talk back—that both calls for and justifies empirical science. Fundamentally, empirical science is an enterprise that seeks to develop images and conceptions that can successfully handle and accommodate the resistance offered by the empirical world under study. The recognition that the empirical world has an obdurate character with which one has to come to terms gives full justification to the realist's insistence that the empirical world has a "real" character. (pp. 22-23)

Even the participant observer's firsthand acquaintance with the empirical world can produce only concepts, pictures, or images of that world. But these concepts are scientific; they "can successfully handle and accommodate the resistance offered by the empirical world." Thus for Blumer what finally characterizes scientific concepts as successful is their demonstrated difference from commonsense concepts. While commonsense concepts are "detached and disparate," scientific concepts are "interrelated and linked," showing "a strain toward consistence" (p. 162). Commonsense concepts are "more static, more persistent with content unchanged" (p. 162), but scientific concepts change. Scientific concepts, that is, "have a career" (p. 161). It is participant observation that gives the scientific concept a career; it is participant observation that demonstrates the difference between common sense and science.

Thus participant observation is to put common sense to the test by making common sense into sensitizing concepts that may or may not prove to be effective. For Blumer, a concept is effective if it functions to make activity possible by enhancing perception.

The conception, in filling the deficiency in perception, not only provides new orientation and releases activity but directs such activity either effectively or ineffectively. The success of the activity to which it gives rise becomes the test of the effectiveness of the concept. The concept is thus bounded on one side by frustrated activity and on the other by consequences which arise from the activity to which it gives direction. In so far as it lies between these portions of an act it has the characteristics of a tool. At first, like all tools, it may be crude and may be used quite experimentally; later, like perfected tools, it may become refined and its use quite standardized. (p. 166)

Scientific concepts, therefore, derive from the demonstration of a "progressive refinement of sensitizing concepts" (p. 151), a demonstration of the effectiveness of science over common sense, in accommodating the obstacles with which the empirical world supposedly frustrates (research) activity.

It would seem, then, that the production of scientific concepts is not merely a matter of faithfully depicting the empirical world, but of depicting it in a way that allows for action, makes action possible or visible as "common property," as Blumer describes it. In this sense, depiction is nearly indistinguishable from the concept in that the concept "permits one to catch and hold some content of experience and make common property of it" (p. 158). Depiction and conception are both effect and production of the same or common point of view, the same or common orientation that makes activity social or collective. As Blumer puts it:

By reason of its verbal or symbolic character, the concept may become an item of social discourse and so permit the conception that it embodies to become common property. A concept always arises as an individual experience, to bridge a gap or insufficiency in perception. In becoming social property it permits others to gain the same point of view and employ the same orientation. As such it enables collective action—a function of the concept which, curiously enough, has received little attention. It is by reason of the fact that the concept is an item of social discourse that concerted procedure is possible as far as science is concerned, and that a structure of science may emerge in place of a mere assemblage of disconnected actions. (pp. 159-160)

A depiction of the empirical world, therefore, allows for collective action when it makes points of view public or when it makes them social property. Thus the whole meaning of participant observation, as Blumer describes it, is to enable the researcher to take the points of view of those he studies, as if to see through their eyes, thereby making their viewpoints common property.

> The research scholar who is concerned with the social action of a given individual or group, or with a given type of social action, must see that action from the position of whoever is forming the action. He should trace the formation of the action in the way in which it is actually formed. This means seeing the situation as it is seen by the actor. (p. 56)
>
> This procedure is to approach the study of group activity through the eyes and experience of the people who have developed the activity. Hence, it necessarily requires an intimate familiarity with this experience and with the scenes of its operation. (p. 139)

If the participant observer is to grasp the actors' points of view so as to make them public, these viewpoints must be depicted in terms of social action. That is, points of view must be depicted as "lines of definition" that show their function in bringing frustrated activity to its realization. Thus the depiction of the empirical world must necessarily enact the transformative effect(iveness) of points of view. Points of view must be interchanged, brought into interaction, if finally their depiction is to demonstrate the change of common sense into science. Each point of view, that is, must be made social property, as the interaction of points of view is shown to make up the gap in perception or the insufficiency of any one point of view. Thus the interaction of points of view must finally yield to a totalizing or common viewpoint from which to see the whole process of conception from the frustration of action to the realization of "social action."

If, then, Blumer argues that only the common viewpoint of science can provide a depiction of the empirical world as it really is, it is, however, the depiction itself that constructs a common viewpoint. Thus the depiction of the empirical world must always also be a reconstruction of its own point of view, a reconstruction of scientific conception. The depiction of the empirical world must reconstruct a struggle to gain a common point of view, a struggle to overcome the insufficiency of perception, a struggle to interchange individual points of view for a common or totalizing viewpoint, or what Blumer describes as the "valid" viewpoint of science (p. 33). Thus the discourse on participant observation methodology necessarily comes to focus on the participant observer himself, and on his struggle to overcome the gap in his perception, a struggle to socialize his perception or point of view. It is the narration of his struggle that allows the depiction of the empirical world also to be a narrative reconstruction of scientific conception.

If the participant observer is to depict the empirical world through the eyes of those he observes, he must do so by narrating his own struggle to gain the common or totalizing vision of science, a struggle to realize his identity in gaining an author(izing) vision. Thus it is through his eyes that both the insufficiency of any one point of view and the effectiveness of a common viewpoint must be demonstrated. It is finally in the unity of his identity (I/eye) that the actors' viewpoints (I's/eyes) provide coherence to scientific conception. Thus what Blumer understands as the obdurate or real character of the empirical world is an effect of the narrative production of the observer's struggle for a unified identity.

While Blumer's writings on methodology all but reveal that the scientific concept is a narrative production and that the coherence and interrelatedness that he claims characterize scientific knowledge are formal effects of narrativity, effects of images and conceptions of the empirical world, his emphasis on the participant observer nevertheless allows the empirical world to remain seemingly independent of concepts and images. That is, attention is shifted away from the narrative production of the scientific concept, focusing instead on the subject of the narrative—the participant observer in his struggle for vision. Further, it is through the narration of the observer's struggle that the depiction of the empirical world embeds a totalizing viewpoint (what feminist film theorists describe as the gaze) with which the viewer can see the world as real, as obdurate, that is, to see with the common viewpoint of science. Thus the narration of the observer's struggles is also marked with a denial of the very relationship it reveals, of desire, narrativity, and authority in the construction of scientific vision.

In what follows, I want to suggest that the discourse on participant observation, like cinematic realism, makes reference to the heroic masculine subject of vision in order to construct narratively a look with which to see the real. It is the figure of the heroic masculine subject that also allows for the disavowal of desire and the productivity of narrativity. I want first to characterize cinematic realism in the terms that feminist film critics provide, in order then to return to the participant observer's struggle, making clearer the oedipal logic of its organization.

CINEMATIC REALISM AND THE PRODUCTION OF "THE LOOK"

While there is no discussion of the relationship of desire to imaging in Blumer's proposal of a participant observation methodology, in his study of the movies Blumer does notice how images, pictures, and concepts depict reality by positioning the viewer in a narrative plot or scenario of desire. Thus Blumer (1933) explains reactions of moviegoers in terms of "emotional possession":

Emotional possession refers to experiences wherein impulses which are ordinarily restrained are strongly stimulated. . . . The individual identifies himself so thoroughly with the plot or loses himself so much in the picture that he is carried away from the usual trend of conduct. His mind becomes fixed on certain imagery, and impulses usually latent or kept under restraint gain expression or seriously threaten to gain such expression. (p. 74)

While Blumer recognizes that viewers can differently interpret filmic images, the overall sense of the motion picture that he conveys is that movies have nearly an unmediated impact on viewers.

Images are supplied, so to speak, ready-made. They have a vividness and a clean-cut character which makes easier their absorption in a "whole cloth" fashion. (p. 189)

Blumer argues that viewers can "secure from movies not only images of this or that object, of this or that form of life, but also a plot, of action, and so to speak, of the movement of life" (p. 188). If the viewer becomes lost in the picture, it is because "before his eyes are displayed modes of living and schemes of conduct which are of the character of his desires and which offer possibilities of instructing him in his own behavior" (p. 195). Blumer concludes that "motion pictures organize [the viewer's] needs and suggest lines of conduct useful for their satisfaction" (p. 195).

Blumer's description of movies is similar to descriptions offered by feminist film critics. In her analysis of the cinematic realism of classical Hollywood cinema, Annette Kuhn (1982) draws on Louis Althusser's (1971) discussion of ideology to argue that

one of the marks of classic Hollywood cinema is the invisibility of its devices of meaning construction: the audience is on the whole not aware

of processes of signification. . . . . Because in dominant cinema meaning
presents itself as 'already there' in the film text, the viewing subject is
positioned as recipient of apparently preconstructed meanings. This is the
ground of the argument that it is the work of ideology to produce an
appearance of wholeness and 'already there-ness' on behalf of the subject.
(pp. 52-53)

Laura Mulvey (1975) suggests:

Playing on the tension between film as controlling the dimension of time
(editing, narrative) and film as controlling the dimension of space (changes
in distance, editing), cinematic codes create a gaze, a world, and an object,
thereby producing an illusion cut to the measure of desire. (p. 427)

Although similar to Blumer's descriptions of the movies, feminist
criticism differs in that it focuses on the "invisible devices of meaning
construction"; the emphasis is on filmic textuality and the way it constructs a subject positionality with which the viewer "sees." Feminist
film criticism therefore suggests a general understanding of realist imaging, proposing that all realist representation embeds a totalizing point
of view as well as subjective positionalities, the formal construction of
which is necessarily disavowed.

If, then, the empirical world can be seen to have an obdurate or real
character, it is because realist imaging gives the empirical world an
appearance of wholeness or already there-ness, composed in relationship to desire. Scenes are constructed so that what is seen is seen as if
from a subject's point of view that is nonetheless resistant to the subject,
that is, that is also seen from a totalizing viewpoint. In cinematic realism,
a totalizing viewpoint seemingly transcends the various subjective points
of view; these viewpoints become conflated with the gaze, or at least
try to appropriate its totalizing transcendence. Vision is thereby organized through the construction of subject positionalities through which
the viewer's unconscious identification is elicited and subjugated to or
in the gaze.

Feminist film critics therefore argue that filmic texts inscribe subjectivity or subject positionalities in the "figure of the spectator." As Mary
Ann Doane (1987) puts it:

Subjectivity is inscribed in the cinema in various ways—through voice-
over, point of view structures, etc.—but it is always localized. . . . Subjec-

tivity in the cinema (the inscription of the "I") is hence displaced from the producer of the discourse to its receiver. In film, there is a curious operation by means of which the "I" and the "you" of discourse are collapsed in the figure of the spectator. (p. 10)

In its displacement of subjectivity from the producer to the receiver, the figure of the spectator allows the viewer to see what is seen as intelligible, as reality. As Teresa De Lauretis (1984) argues:

> The spectator, stitched in the film's spatio-temporal movement, is constructed as the point of intelligibility and origin of these representations, as the subject of, the "figure-for," those images and meanings. (p. 53)

If, then, cinematic realism gives an appearance of wholeness and completeness to the empirical world, it is by giving the viewer a sense of wholeness and completeness in vision. Therefore, unlike Blumer's proposal that empirical reality stands against images and pictures of it, feminist film criticism proposes that it is realist representation itself that makes what is seen seem real, makes it believable in its opposition to the individual's imaging. The interchange of individuals' points of view, which Blumer argues constitutes an adequate representation of the empirical world, is understood within feminist criticism to be an effect of realist representation itself—the displacement of subjectivity from producer to receiver only appearing as an interaction of subjective perspectives. Rather than making up what is lacking in any individual's imaging, cinematic realism disavows lack in and for the subject. In conflating subject positionalities with the gaze, cinematic realism offers the viewer an imaginary unified subject identity, constructed in a fantasy of visual mastery over what the subject seemingly lacks. Condensing a desire for a lost wholeness or completeness, the figure of the spectator elicits the viewer's desire for a unified identity.

For feminist film critics, cinematic realism exemplifies the workings of unconscious desire, just as the workings of unconscious desire imply many of the strategies with which realism tries to overcome the threats to its own coherence, such as the loss of the real in realist representation as well as the loss of the writer and reader or viewer to abstracted textual forms of authority. To understand these losses and their disavowal in cinematic realism, feminist critics draw on what I have already described as the psychoanalytic understanding of the subject's constitution through separations and losses, in particular, the separation from

and the loss of the mother. Feminist film criticism especially makes use
of a psychoanalytic understanding of fantasies as (post-)oedipal defenses
against loss in which the subject appropriates the phallic function by
displacing the losses onto the feminine figure as "her" castration. Thus
the implied reduction of sexual difference to a crude anatomical opposition in the fantasmatic construction of a unified subject identity not
only privileges the phallus, but implies that the feminine figure be kept
under surveillance, be kept in sight as the figure of castration.

Thus, while Freud specifically discussed defensive fantasies against
castration in terms of the masculine subject's response to the woman's
castration, feminist film critics suggest that these fantasies are what
Kaja Silverman (1988, p. 31) describes as "secondary constructions,"
in that the masculine subject's first defensive construction is to project
his losses onto the feminine figure, which thereby comes to figure "his"
losses or castrations, but as "hers." Therefore, these secondary fantasmatic constructions, seemingly aimed at mastering her castration, must
necessarily also focus on controlling vision and visibility. The reduction
of sexual difference to a crude anatomical opposition is thereby regis-
tered in terms of the gaze, as the masculine figure seemingly appropriates the gaze by being identified as the one who sees or controls vision,
and the feminine figure is identified as the one who is seen or is controlled in or by vision. Thus, by providing what Silverman describes as
"a range of defensive operations to be used against the image of woman,
from disavowal and fetishism to voyeurism and sadism" (p. 31), cinematic realism informs strategies of knowledge/power with an authorizing gaze, a totalizing viewpoint, constituted of fantasmatic secondary
constructs.

Thus the totalizing viewpoint that the figure of the spectator embeds
in realist representation is constructed as authoritative (or to have the
phallic function) by restaging in representation itself the masculine subject's struggle for a unified identity. This struggle is specifically enacted
in terms of the secondary defenses of vision, that is, in terms of fantasmatic scenarios in which the castrated figure is visually controlled
either through a fetishistic idealization or by a subjugation to a sadistic
punishment. And if these scenarios of sexual desire initiate the viewer
into the very movement of the look, the very movement of realist representation, it is because a prior identification, as De Lauretis (1984, p.
144) puts it, is elicited of the viewer, an identification with the figures
of the narrative: the masculine figure of heroic action and the feminine
figure of obstacles or resistance. Thus the construction of the gaze in

cinematic realism leans on the figures of narrativity. Identification with both figures is necessary for the viewer to see. As De Lauretis argues:

> The figural narrative identification . . . is double; both figures can and in fact must be identified with at once, for they are inherent in narrativity itself. It is this narrative identification that assures "the hold of the image," the anchoring of the subject in the flow of the film's movement. (p. 144)

If, then, the viewer is to take the totalizing viewpoint that realist representation offers, it is through identifications with the figures of the narrative. The narrative figures also put the viewer's "fantasmatic" into play, which generates what Silverman (1988) describes as

> erotic tableaux or *combinatoires* in which the subject is arrestingly positioned—whose function is, in fact, precisely to display the subject in a given place. Its original cast of characters would seem to be drawn from the familial reserve, but in the endless secondary productions to which the fantasmatic gives rise, all actors but one are frequently recast. And even that one constant player may assume different roles on different occasions. (p. 216)

There is then a deep connection between the narrative construction of the gaze and the persistence in the unconscious of a failed sexual identity, which after all is what permits the viewer to take various subject positionalities in the first place.

So while narrativity puts unconscious desire into play, narrativity can and usually does limit the play of the unconscious when finally identities are fixed. Thus, in the end, when the masculine subject realizes himself as the subject of vision, having seemingly regained control in terms of the fantasmatic defenses against the feminine figure, a distinction is obtained between the subject who sees and the spectacularized other that is seen. The masculine subject prevails as the author of vision(s), having all but lost himself in the feminine figure of the spectacle, that is, the figure of what is not yet known, what is not yet spoken, what is not yet envisioned.

If, since the eighteenth century, realist representation authorizes empirical scientific knowledge by the erasure in the representation of the reader and writer or viewer, realist representation also narrates the subject's struggle to appropriate the phallic function. In cinematic realism, the struggle ends with the masculine subject's mastering vision by holding the feminine figure in sight rather than himself. Thus cinematic realism is the culmination of the realist project begun in the eighteenth century; as Silverman (1988) argues, "Over the past two centuries, the male subject has increasingly dissociated himself from the visible attempting thereby to align himself with a symbolic order within which power has become more and more dispersed and dematerial" (p. 26). Thus the masculine subject has appropriated power by dissociating himself from the spectacularized others of vision and not by simply denying their presence or their visions but by making their points of view public only through and as his vision.

If, then, the gaze of cinematic realism is often described to provide "a passive, affectless way of seeing" (Spiegel 1976, p. 82; see also Cavell 1979; Bruss 1980) or a way of seeing characterized by "a sexless objectivity" (Chatman 1980, p. 132), it is because the scenarios of sexual desire that inform cinematic realism allow for the disavowal of desire, displacing the vulnerabilities of vision onto the feminine figure, so to disburden the masculine subject of the necessary losses of subjectivity. The seeming sexless objectivity of realist representation of the empirical world derives from a naturalization of the fantasmatic reduction of sexual difference to a crude anatomical opposition operated through the narrative reconstruction of the subject's struggle to master vision.

WRITING FROM THE
POSITION OF THE OUTSIDER

If the discourse on participant observation informs empirical social science with the capacity for an authorized vision, it is by grounding research in the narrative reconstruction of the observer's struggle for vision. However, while this struggle must be made visible in realist representation of the empirical world, finally the researcher must seemingly be absented from that representation. That is, since the researcher must present the empirical world only through the eyes of those he observes, the researcher must finally displace his own viewpoint; he must seemingly exchange his viewpoint for theirs. Therefore, the narration of the observer's struggle must dramatize the researcher's resisting his own point of view or any partial point of view, a resistance that Blumer (1969) argues is central to empirical social science:

Research scholars, like human beings in general, are slaves to their own pre-established images and thus are prone to assume that other people see the given objects as they, the scholars see them. Scholars need to guard against this proneness and to give high priority to deliberate testing of their images. (p. 52)

If for the researcher the purpose of participant observation is to test his own images deliberately, then the narration of the observer's struggles must demonstrate his moving from what Blumer describes as "the position of the outsider" in order to get "in close touch with the action and experiences of the people who are involved" (p. 35). Thus the narration of the observer's struggle comes to be thematized in terms of getting in and out of close touch with the observed. As Blumer puts it:

The metaphor that I like is that of lifting the veils that obscure or hide what is going on. The task of scientific study is to lift the veils that cover the area of group life that one proposes to study. . . . The veils are lifted by getting close to the area and by digging deep into it through careful study. . . . This is not a simple matter of just approaching a given area and looking at it. It is a tough job requiring a high order of careful and honest probing. . . . It is not "soft" study. (p. 40)

The narration of participant observation thus turns from the researcher's struggle with his own images to focus on his struggle against the resistance that the empirical world seemingly offers. The struggle becomes a struggle to see more than mere perception allows, to see deeply, beneath the veil with which the empirical world supposedly hides itself. Thus what is first understood as the researcher's struggle with his imaging is displaced onto the spectacle itself. Now it is the spectacle that is difficult, that is resistant to penetration. The spectacle now threatens with castration, so that what comes to motivate participant observation is the desire to get as close as possible to what is observed without getting lost in it, without becoming completely absorbed in what is to be made visible.

Thus, in its narration, participant observation becomes eroticized with the anxiety and excitement of the sexual scenarios of vision. These scenarios, Mark Seltzer (1987) argues, are central to realist representation, as they narratively reconstruct the observer's struggle for vision as a struggle against "risks and vulnerabilities of a deep engagement at once visual and bodily" (p. 85). Thus what appears to Blumer as the empirical world's resistance to the observer's look is narratively constructed as the observer's projection outward of his resistance to the "pleasures of seeing," which disrupt "the power of seeing" as "the very absorption in, even intoxication with seeing opens the possibility of violent loss of balance or disempowerment" (p. 85). In the narration of participant observation, the focus shifts away from the researcher's struggle with his own images to a struggle with the observed, now figured as the feminine threat of castration and (re)absorption.

Marking the site of observation as feminine gives a certain meaning to the narration of observation, as the observer is seen to inhabit the site, even to become identified with it or all but lost to it. The observer thereby becomes the object of the gaze, enacting what Stanley Cavell (1979) describes as the "wish not to need power" (p. 41), which in cinematic realism is usually embodied in the figure who occupies the passive position, the feminine figure who is to be looked at. Thus the observer identifies with the feminine figure at least temporarily, making himself visible as suffering the viewpoints of other actors. He gives assurance that he has gotten deep inside, close enough without becoming fully absorbed in the spectacle. Figuring the site of observation as feminine informs the observer's struggle with a thematics of a seemingly natural repulsion, the revulsion of the maternal body that the feminine figure usually connotes. The observer's leaving the site thereby becomes necessary but mournful and therefore heroic. Thus, when the observer removes himself from the site in order to again inhabit the outsider's position, his leaving underwrites his observations with a sexless objectivity. That is, he is finally seen as distinct from the feminine figure, reidentified with the active masculine position, naturalized as sexless.

But leaving the scene of observation only puts the observer at the scene of writing. While Blumer imagines the observer digging deep into the empirical world, it is difficult to imagine the tool, the conceptual tool, with which Blumer suggests the observer dig without imagining it as an instrument of writing, the writing tool that cuts into the virgin, blank page and upon which the writer leaves the mark of writing or of a writing technology. Thus it is hard not to imagine the veil, which appears to Blumer as part of the natural resistance of the empirical world, to be, rather, a function of writing—an imagined veil permitting approach by concealing the horror of being absorbed in the spectacle.

The horror of the spectacle is always already the horror of the becoming visible of writing. In his analysis of realist representation, Michael Fried (1987) argues that in texts that are meant "by the power of the written word . . . to make you see," what is not to be seen is writing; what is not to be scened is the writer's writing (p. 79). Such texts necessarily enact a strategy for the denial of writing's productivity, the denial of the narrative production of the gaze. Thus the identification of the observer with the feminine figure of the observed finally works in the disavowal of writing and the productivity of narrativity. The observer is presented as if he were subjugated in and to other subjects' points of view, as if his observations were spoken by them and thus written by them. The writer can present himself as merely transmitting what participant observation made of the observer, how it made him a hero, from whom the writer is humbly distanced and thereby finally absented from the representation.

It is this strategy of denial that is constituted as a mass medium in the early development of narrative cinema. Thus, just as in cinematic realism, the narrative reconstruction of the observer's struggle for vision provides realist representation with an authorizing narrativity that Doane (1987) argues is necessary to "balancing knowledge and belief in relation to the reality status of the image" (p. 14). That is, although the viewer knows the image is only an image, he believes in "the impression of reality" that the image produces, "in order to follow the story" (p. 15). It is the narrative of the observer's struggle that gives a sense to the empirical world as having an integrity inherent to it, even while understanding it as such requires the hard work of the individual's interpretation, reading, and writing. Thus the realist representation deriving from participant observation gives what Alan Spiegel (1976) describes for cinematic representation as "an impression of the visible world as . . . other than, remote from, and resistant to, the human mind" while at the same time shifting the emphasis "from the object seen to the seer seeing" (p. 82). Thus cinematic realism, like the discourse on participant observation, allows for an objective vision of the empirical world from a subjective point of view, by finally identifying that subjective point of view with the totalizing viewpoint of the narrative itself.

Michael Schudson (1978) argues that in the 1920s and the 1930s "the discourses of factuality" distinguished themselves by making claim to an "ideal of objectivity" (p. 122). This ideal, Schudson proposes, arises not as an "extension of naive empiricism" but rather as a reaction to the felt impossibility of meeting the claims of naive empiricism, which Schudson traces to a post-World War I skepticism about democracy and the market economy, as well as to the growing realization of the manipulative capacities of the mass media, advertising, and marketing, a disillusioning realization in which the movies played no small part (Ewen 1976). In that same period and against his own findings about the movies, Blumer codified the naturalistic methodology of participant observation. With it, he informed empirical social science with an ideal of objectivity that was informed with a skepticism about images, conceptions, and pictures. Rather than resolving the anxiety about images and pictures, however, the discourse on participant observation methodology represses it, since its ideal of objectivity is enacted with a narrativity itself informed with a cinematic realism. Hence the anxiety about images and pictures will return again and again to trouble the discourse on participant observation, as it does in realism generally.

NOTE

1. The references to Blumer's writings are drawn from the 1969 collection of his papers. I have quoted not only from the long first review essay appearing in that volume but from other papers in that volume that first appeared between 1930 and 1956. Information on the original publications appears in the references. Blumer wrote about methodology as early as 1928 in his unpublished dissertation, *Method in Social Psychology.* Ideas first formulated there are developed in his later writings.

REFERENCES

Althusser, Louis. 1971. *Lenin and Philosophy.* New York: Monthly Review Press.
Becker, Howard. 1988. "Herbert Blumer's Conceptual Impact." *Symbolic Interaction* 11 (Spring): 13-21.
Blumer, Herbert. 1931. "Science Without Concepts." *American Journal of Sociology* 36: 515-533.
———. 1933. *Movies and Conduct.* New York: Macmillan.
———. 1954. "What's Wrong with Social Theory." *American Sociological Review* 19.
———. 1956. "Sociological Analysis and the 'Variable.' " *American Sociological Review* 21: 683-690.
———. 1969. *Symbolic Interactionism.* Englewood Cliffs, NJ: Prentice-Hall.
Bruss, Elizabeth. 1980. "Eye for I: Making and Unmaking Autobiography in Film." In *Autobiography: Essays Theoretical and Critical,* edited by James Olney. Princeton, NJ: Princeton University Press.
Cavell, Stanley. 1979. *The World Viewed.* Cambridge, MA: Harvard University Press.
Chatman, Seymour. 1980. "What Novels Can Do That Films Can't (and Vice Versa)." *Critical Inquiry* 7: 121-140.
De Lauretis, Teresa. 1984. *Alice Doesn't: Feminism, Semiotics, Cinema.* Bloomington: Indiana University Press.

Doane, Mary Ann. 1987. *The Desire to Desire*. Bloomington: Indiana University Press.

Ewen, Stuart. 1976. *Captains of Consciousness*. New York: McGraw-Hill.

Fried, Michael. 1987. *Realism, Writing, Disfiguration*. Chicago: University of Chicago Press.

Kuhn, Annette. 1982. *Women's Pictures*. London: Routledge & Kegan Paul.

Lemert, Charles. 1979. *Sociology and the Twilight of Man*. Carbondale: Southern Illinois University Press.

Mulvey, Laura. 1975. "Visual Pleasure and Narrative Cinema." *Screen* 16: 6-18.

Schudson, Michael. 1978. *Discovering the News*. New York: Basic Books.

Seltzer, Mark. 1987. "Statistical Persons." *Diacritics* 17(Fall): 82-98.

Silverman, Kaja. 1988. *The Acoustic Mirror: The Female Voice in Psychoanalysis and Cinema*. Bloomington: Indiana University Press.

Spiegel, Alan. 1976. *Fiction and the Camera Eye*. Charlottesville; University Press of Virginia.

3

THE FIGURE OF THE WOMAN
IN THE NATURALIST MACHINE

Technology always has been about the maternal body and it does seem to be about some kind of male phantasm—but, more, it perceives that the machine *is* a woman in that phantasm. (Jardine 1987, p. 156)

The cyborg is a matter of fiction and lived experience that changes what counts as women's experience in the late twentieth century. This is a struggle over life and death, but the boundary between science fiction and social reality is an optical illusion. (Haraway 1985a, p. 66)

If in narrative closure the final hero is figured as masculine, it is because he has mastered the threats posed by the other; he has brought about change or made something happen to (an)other. There is, then, as Laura Mulvey (1975) notices, something of a relationship between narrativity and sadomasochism: "Sadism demands a story, depends on making something happen, forcing a change in another person, a battle of will and strength, victory/defeat, all occurring in a linear time with a beginning and an end" (p. 14). Given that the other is usually figured as feminine or as a woman, it is the feminine figure or the woman who must suffer

---

Author's Note: This chapter, titled " 'The Final Girl' in the Fictions of Science and Culture," is to appear in an upcoming issue of the *Stanford Humanities Review*.

change. Thus the relationship of narrativity and sadomasochism often implies an enactment of the woman's coming to or being brought to femininity, as femininity is reduced to passivity and masochism to femininity. Thus the relationship of sadomasochism and narrativity often implies the final reduction of sexual difference to a crude anatomical opposition that also serves in configuring sociological roles as well.

If such a reduction serves narrative resolution, it does so by defensively misrepresenting sadomasochism. After all, Freud (1962) argues that "the most remarkable feature" of sadomasochism is "that its active and passive forms are habitually found to occur together in the same individual," showing the "simultaneous presence" of "masculinity and femininity, activity and passivity" (pp. 25-26). If, then, in narrative closure the masculine subject's heroics are defined and valorized, by finally reducing femininity to passivity and masochism to femininity, it is to allow sadomasochistic scenarios of sexual desire both to elicit the play of unconscious desire in terms of a failed sexual identity and to defend finally against failed identity in a reduction of sexual difference to a crude anatomical opposition.

But if the would-be hero is a woman, it might be expected that the narrative means to sustain the perverse pleasure of turning passivity and activity one into the other, to sustain the horror of the indefinite mix-up of masculinity and femininity, pleasure and pain. Indeed, the "final girl," as Carol Clover (1987) describes the heroine of "slasher films," bodies forth a questionable mix-up of masculinity and femininity in the service of a pleasurable pain. While "inevitably female," the final girl is nonetheless "boyish." She is the one who is "chased, cornered, wounded," the one living with the knowledge "of the preceding horror and of her own peril" (p. 210). Yet her "smartness, gravity, competence in mechanical and other matters," her seeming sexual indifference, set her apart from other females (p. 204). Clover argues that at least in slasher films, the final girl represents an easing of the equation of anatomy and sexual identity, registering changes brought on by "the women's movement, the entry of women into the workplace, and the rise of divorce and woman-headed families" (p. 220).

But if the final girl can register a reconfiguration of sociological roles, her appearance may also function to restore the relationship of realism and an oedipal logic of narrativity, while adjusting it to the changes femininity and masculinity will have to figure. Thus the final girl may make possible the recruitment of a new media to function for a writing technology of the subject in terms of changed political, economic arrangements.

In this chapter, I offer rereadings of *Alien* and *Gorillas in the Mist* to trace the narrative of two would-be final girls. The narrativization of the women's heroic ordeals functions in these films to reshape the relations of knowledge/power in terms of computer technology by reconfiguring the oppositions and relays between fact and fiction, nature and environment, self and society, sexuality and economy, private and public. If, in *Gorillas in the Mist*, Dian Fossey dies in order to secure empirical knowledge in a romantic version of science's past, in *Alien*, Ripley lives to face endless ordeals, giving science a future, while intensifying sadomasochistic pleasure with which the movie viewer is introduced to the delights of computer use.

NARRATING A PAST FOR SCIENCE'S FUTURE

In *Gorillas in the Mist*, Dian Fossey, having left behind her fiancé, arrives in the Belgian Congo only to find herself soon in the middle of a revolution for independence. Discouraged by this setback to her research, Fossey finally begins again in Rwanda. There, she is eventually joined by a photographer from *National Geographic*. After a passionate love affair he proposes marriage, but she refuses to leave "her" gorillas, which the marriage seemingly would entail. When the photographer leaves, Fossey continues her research and relentlessly battles the local government and local people to prevent the killing of the gorillas for the sale of the animals' parts. Other than working, Dian Fossey seems to do nothing but smoke and drink excessively. Finally, she is murdered; her murderer, a mystery. She is buried by Zimbagaree, her African guide, next to Digit, Fossey's favorite of the silverbacks. Zimbagaree connects two lines of stones that surround the graves, allowing the spirits of Digit and Fossey to be together for eternity.

Portrayed as the weird obsession of "an amazing woman," scientific research is made to seem all the more demanding. But if Dian Fossey's life and work appear to insist on the necessity of the oppositions of science and sexuality, science and domesticity, science and political economy, it is these very oppositions that seem to bring on the degeneration of Fossey's character, deforming the life of the woman too much alone, through alcohol, cigarettes, and excessive involvement in politics. In the figure of the woman researcher, then, the rigors of science are reenacted, but Fossey's failures finally suggest that the version of science characterized by the heroic independence of the lone researcher can only be treated now as womanly, utterly romantic in a nostalgic history of science, Africa, and the ape.

The end of the story must be the end of Dian Fossey's life, not so much to guarantee the future of scientific research in the detachment and objectivity of the scientist, but to ensure an object and a space that signify the shared origin of science and man, an origin outside both: the surviving ape, the research object in its "natural habitat," Africa, the site of the white man's prehistory. But if the foundations of science can only now be underwritten with a story that romanticizes the past, it is because the future of science has become a purely practical matter.

To speak practically of science's future is to speak not in terms of the independence of its researchers, but rather of science's coming to terms with a system of political, economic relationships. In *Alien,* Ripley is a crew member on a commercial towing vessel, the *Nostromo.* The spaceship is on its way home with a cargo of 20 million tons of mineral ore when, unexpectedly, the Company, the conglomerate that owns the vessel, requests that the ship land on a planetoid that has reported a dangerous presence. The crew knows nothing of the alien, but the Company does and hopes to recover it in order to sell it as a weapon to the military. The Company has programmed the *Nostromo's* computer, called Mother, so that the ship's first priority, over the crew's safety, is the return of the alien. The science officer, Ash, is an android planted on the ship by the Company, again unknown to the crew (and the audience). Ash is faithful to the Company's morally reprehensible strategy of accumulating profits and knowledge.

It is the Company that is responsible for Ripley's confrontation with the alien, which mirrors the Company's own greed:

> Late twentieth-century capitalism, with its unslakable thirst to propagate its vast institutions, is nominated as the sinister force which has reincarnated the omnipotent beast. The condemnation of a callous, consumerist ethos, obliquely set forth in *The Texas Chainsaw Massacre* and the Romero *Dead* opera, now emerges undisguised. The company, playing out its intergalactic scenario of contemporary corporate smash-and-grab, is emphatically labelled villainous; the Alien recognized as avatar of its unholy scavenging. (Greenberg 1986, pp. 105-106)

But if *Alien* suggests that late capitalism is the villainous cause of the lost ideals of scientific objectivity and autonomy, the distinctions that

Ripley's heroics are meant to set in place are not a matter of reconstituting an institutional domain of disinterested knowledge. *Alien,* rather, "assails the audience with that same spirit of negativity, destructiveness, and exploitation" that the movie criticizes as characteristic of the Company (Greenberg 1986, p. 107). All institutions seem enmeshed in profit making and power brokering. All are made indistinguishable from one another by their mutual investment in transinstitutional systems of information storage and retrieval.

The heroics of the lone ethnographer in a land elsewhere, who struggles to sustain integrity, which in the end accrues authority to the institutional establishment, is no longer an empowering vision of knowledge. Thus Ripley is a heroine not so much because of her integrity but because she is just smart enough to survive. In her struggle to outwit the Company and its Mother computer, so to free herself from the alien, Ripley functions alongside the destructiveness and exploitation of the Company. She figures knowledge as a personal sensitivity, alternately mystical and paranoid, having abandoned any expectation of objective and institutional confirmation of her sense(s).

Thus, if Dian Fossey is killed in the name of nostalgia for a scientific authority based on the scientist's integrity and autonomy, Ripley figures a science that functions without nostalgia. Science is, rather, embedded in a set of relations among capital, the state, and the military that science itself helps to shape. It would seem that it is no longer a matter of science's subjugation to these, but of the alliances science forges in constituting relations of power/knowledge.

However, if in *Alien* science and technology are at first presented as monstrous with inhuman priorities, in the end they appear friendlier than the monstrous alien. I want to propose that the alien represents a writing technology-out-of-control, and Ripley's victory over it serves to domesticate the technology that the alien represents. *Alien* reenacts a narrative strategy that naturalizes the excesses of the machine, figuring them as the excesses of feminine sexuality, and thus provoking a need for male-dominated systems of control.

THE FIGURE OF THE WOMAN
AND THE NATURALIST MACHINE

In describing the narrative strategy of the nineteenth-century naturalist novel as "the naturalist machine," Mark Seltzer (1986) sees the naturalist novel as an intensified extension of what I have been referring to as the oedipal logic of realist narrativity. Thus the naturalist novel makes clear how realist narrativity chiasmically holds together elements from opposed registers, such as body and machine, nature and environment, private and public, economy and sexuality, so that "a more or less efficient, more or less effective system of transformations and relays between 'opposed' and contradictory registers" is gradually elaborated (p. 136). What appears to be a resolve of contradictions is rather "a flexible mechanism of adjustments . . . , intrinsically promoting a coordination of conflicting practices, while strategically preserving the differences between these practices" (p. 136). Each adjustment is part of a regulation of difference, which the narrative operates through an oedipal logic of sexual difference.

Thus the naturalist machinery of the nineteenth-century novel was often worked through a story in which the mother's body was made a figure of "natural" production. Positively contrasted with machine production, at least at first, the mother's body served as a defense against the crisis of the overproduction of a technology seemingly out of control. But finally the mother's body becomes the site of an "unmanning fecundity," effected in the degeneration of the man-made father or the mother's death. Her sexuality now representing a production out of control, the mother's excesses are made to support a moral reinvestment in a reorganized, crisis-managed male-dominated machine production— her excesses domesticating those of the machine.

> The colossal mother is thus rewritten as a machine of force that brings men into the world, "the symphony of reproduction" as "the colossal pendulum of an almighty machine." And crucially, if the mother is merely a "carrier" of force, the mother herself is merely a medium—midwife and middleman—of the force of generation. (Seltzer 1986, p. 121)

The naturalist machine writes female generativity as a negation of male power and then rewrites it as a negation of the former negation, thus "capitalizing on force as a counter to female generativity in particular and to anxieties about generation and production in general" (p. 121).

In cross-coupling the mother's body and the machine, the naturalist novel not only opposed the production of goods and the production of producers (and consumers), it also provided for discursive and practical relays between them, eventually redefining the opposition of the private and the public. Thus, by the first decades of the twentieth century, women would be expected to be more than biological mothers; they were represented as the prime consumers of images, central to mass production and the developing mass media system of information, marketing, and entertainment (Ewen 1976). But the media posed its own threat as a technology-out-of-control, in proposing the possibility of the collapse of the distinction of image and reality. The early narrative cinema composed itself as a naturalist machine cross-coupling the woman's body with the excesses of mechanically reproduced imagery.

The excesses of the machine were displaced onto the woman, as she became the stereotype of the spectator and as her virtual "spectatorship" became "yet another clearly delineated mark of her excess" (Doane 1987, p. 1).

> For there is a certain naiveté assigned to women in relation to systems of signification—a tendency to deny the processes of representation, to collapse the opposition between the sign (the image) and the real. To "misplace" desire by attaching it too securely to a representation. (Doane 1987, p. 1)

The woman supposedly takes the image so seriously that she tries to become it. As a figure of visual excess, then, the woman is put into play in the naturalist machine of the cinema so as to defuse its excesses as well as those perceived to be hers.

Indeed, in early cinema, as Michael Rogin (1985) argues in an analysis of D. W. Griffith's *The Birth of a Nation,* cinematic imagery "endangered narrative control and threatened chaos. The source of that chaos visible on screen was the female image" (p. 158).

> The New Woman appears everywhere at the end of the nineteenth century, in the work force and reform movements, in literature, art, social thought, and psychology. . . . Whatever her social form, the New Woman was imaged as monstrous and chameleonlike. Her permeable boundaries absorbed children and men. (p. 158)

Through an economy of images, Griffith's camera controlled the woman whose very freedom it materialized. That control was expressed visually and through a narrative plot that first displaces the implied sexual freedom of the woman onto the "freed" black man of post-Civil War reconstruction, who then subjugates the "liberated" woman to his violence. Since the woman is the daughter of a northern politician who had championed the cause of the slaves, Rogin argues that when the daughter is saved by the Ku Klux Klan, she and the nation are released from paternalism, as the father's power is negated and displaced onto corporate structures.

Subjugating the woman on screen, to sexual violence and then to domestication by restriction to her "proper place," was not only a response to the demands of the New Woman of the 1920s, it was also a recontainment of the threat that cinema proposed to the narrative mechanisms by which distinctions are made. Thus the distinction of image and reality that cinema threatened is restored in cinema by the narrative fixing of vision to the castrated maternal body and the containment of its threat by the attribution of beauty to the woman so that "the visual pleasure that body gives to the male now has its basis in ontological security" (Doane 1987, p. 141). In early cinema, then, the image of the woman is made a narrative-producing mechanism, a part of a writing technology of the subject under corporate capitalism. In Fritz Lang's *Metropolis,* the woman as narrative mechanism is actually constructed on screen as a female robotic machine.

The robot has been invented at the request of the master of Metropolis, a futuristic, technological city, in order to agitate disunity among the workers. The workers have been inspired to organize by Maria, a worker's daughter. Although she preaches only hope and patience, her behavior is seen as a threat. The robot is made to resemble Maria exactly, as her body is transferred onto the machine elements by Rotwang, the "diabolic" scientist and inventor.

The robot/Maria is first presented to an all-male group of managers and employers in order to see if they can determine whether the woman who appears before them is a machine. The robot dances a striptease and the men are enthralled. Their fascinated stares are repeated in a frame that shows a montage of many eyes—the men's vision part of the female spectacle that they have constructed. As Andreas Huyssen (1986) argues:

> The montage of male eyes staring at the false Maria . . . illustrates how the male gaze actually constitutes the female body on the screen. It is as if we were witnessing the second, public creation of the robot, her flesh, skin, and body not only being revealed, but constituted by the desire of male vision. (p. 74)

After the workers revolt by refusing to man the city, their homes are flooded, their wives and children suffering most from their rebellion.

The "real" Maria is able to free herself from Rotwang's home and reappears just as the workers, in angry frustration, burn the robot at the stake, revealing the machine beneath its womanly flesh. Since, at the beginning of the film, the master's son had fallen in love with Maria and was also inspired by her to help the workers, his faith in her is now restored, having been so severely challenged by her behavior as the "false" Maria, whom he took to be real.

It is as if the machine is punished both for being an excessively sexual woman and for being the creation of a feminized male, as Rotwang is characterized to be (Dadoun 1986, p. 153). In burning the female flesh of the robot and in the son's victory over Rotwang, who plunges to his death during a struggle with the master's son, the denigration of female sexuality permits the final joining of labor and owner. When, in the end, the son, with Maria at his side, joins his father's hand with that of the foreman, the son comes to embody male power, as the managerial head of an incorporated body of workers, supported by the displacement of female sexuality and the subjugation of scientific knowledge and invention.

If in *The Birth of a Nation* the woman figures in the reshaping of production and consumption in the incorporation of a new mass medium, *Metropolis* shows that the crisis management the medium would come to embody was focused on controlling and channeling vision. The threat of collapsing the distinction of image and reality was displaced onto the woman spectator, who then could be countered in the visual subjugation of the woman by the moving camera. Keeping vision under social and technical control was legitimated in practices that seemingly constrained the sexual pleasures of the desire to see and be seen.

If, then, *Alien* can be said to put the naturalist machine to work once again, it is because it cross-couples the misinforming, hostile Mother computer with the alien and equally threatening figure of the mother's body, in order to domesticate or discipline the excesses of computer technology. The threat that the alien poses well matches the threat of the Mother computer. Described by Ash as a "survivor unclouded by conscience, remorse or delusions of morality," the alien is an egg-laying monstrosity that takes human bodies as the hosts for its eggs. It has various forms, including a phallic form in which it can impale a human with a swordlike appendage. It also constructs uterine, fallopianlike environments in which to preserve its eggs. Because of these characteristics, Barbara Creed (1986) argues, the alien represents the body of the mother both in terms of her pre-oedipal generativity and in terms of castration.

While the image of the castrated mother speaks unequivocally of subjugation to the oedipal logic, the image of the pre-oedipal, generative mother is a fantasmatic construction that means to reject oedipality and castration altogether. This fantasy registers a threat to the oedipal logic of narrativity itself. That is, as the origin of life the generative mother is made a figure that threatens to reabsorb what she has nurtured. She is a devouring, reincorporating figure in which all distinctions are erased between human and inhuman, between life and death, between human and machine, between fact and fiction.

In *Alien,* the male tries to contain the mother's generative function by appropriating it. Kane, one of the crew members, is impregnated by the alien and gives birth, through his stomach, to an infant alien form. But the reproductive terrorism of the alien is not contained. The alien must be ejected completely from the environment in order to rehumanize it. It is a woman, Ripley, who must overcome the alien, so as to defuse, domesticate, or "properly" feminize the out-of-control computer technology that the alien as overproductive mother represents. Eventually, Ripley will represent the computer, in contrast to the generativity of the alien, as friendlier or, at least, necessary to the human. After all, the environment that is rehumanized by the ejection of the alien is a computer-simulated human environment, and in her victorious struggle with the alien, Ripley will be enabled by the use of a computerized life suit (and, in *Aliens,* by a huge robotic mechanism). Ripley's victory over the alien will demonstrate a difference between proper and improper uses of computer technology, as her image comes to negotiate the difference between proper and improper femininity. In the end, Ripley figures a "good" feminine cyborg; the alien, a "bad" one.

Thus if Ripley is, as Constance Penley (1986) argues, "simply the Terminator turned inside out" (p. 77), the attachment of computerized mechanisms to the woman's body seems to make a difference. In *The Terminator,* the cyborg is destroyed by a woman, in order that her son might be born and fulfill the promise of destroying the artificial intelligence that reproduces the terminators. In *The Terminator,* then, technology is refused because its evil is irredeemable. But in *Alien,* Ripley's encounters with the overproductive egg-laying alien suggest, by contrast, the possibility of containing the excesses of computer technology.

Thus Ripley finally rechannels the productivity of computer technology as her image rechannels feminine generativity. If the ejection of the alien serves, as Creed (1986) argues, to "re-draw the boundaries between the human and non-human . . . to separate out the symbolic order from all that threatens its stability, particularly the mother and all that her universe signifies" (p. 53), then Ripley's victory saves the oedipal logic of realist narrativity. It restores the mechanism of reducing difference to oppositions as even the femininity of the "new" woman is reduced to passivity and passivity to a "proper" or appropriated femininity. Thus in the final scene, just before Ripley's last encounter with the alien, she undresses before the camera, seemingly exhibiting herself to the voyeuristic, male gaze. In a film that had been so insistently indifferent to fixed sexual identities, Ripley's display seems remarkable. Creed comments on this scene:

> Compared to the horrific sight of the alien as fetish object of the monstrous feminine, Ripley's body is pleasurable and reassuring to look at. She signifies the "acceptable" form and shape of woman. In a sense the monstrousness of woman, represented by Mother as betrayer (the computer/life support system), and Mother as the uncontrollable, generative, cannibalistic mother (the alien), is controlled through the display of woman as reassuring and pleasurable sign. (p. 69)

In the end, Ripley is the heroine but she no longer is a final girl, a mix of masculinity and femininity. Rather, she has been fixed up, fixed into femininity. This is even more pronounced in *Aliens,* as the femininity of the "new" woman is finally refitted into a reconstructed family, as Ripley saves a little girl and almost certainly threatens her own survival, while a male crew-mate and would-be lover awaits them both. It is in the passive position, domesticated, that Ripley is the appropriate(d) figure to subdue the excesses of computer technology. A heroine is needed, I would propose, in domesticating a technology that not only threatens representation with its simulated realities but is itself so readily connected to the maternal body and new reproductive technologies.

Thus the naturalist machine is a narrative strategy to save realist narrativity for the scientific production of knowledge, while adjusting the oppositions and relays between fact and fiction. If, then, *Alien* is a moment of science fiction that yields finally to a new sense of scientificity, a reconfiguration of science, technology, power, this reconfiguration displaces an earlier moment of science fiction, an earlier version of the story of science, technology, power, a version that *Gorillas in the Mist* represents and thereby retires.

SCIENCE: FROM DIORAMA TO
COMPUTERIZED SIMULATION

In the same years when narrative cinema was being developed and ethnographic participatory observation was being institutionalized as a scientific methodology, the Akeley African Hall of the Museum of Natural History was conceived by Carl Akeley. After hunting in Africa, first with a gun and then with a camera, Akeley designed the dioramas that would be housed in the museum. He also secured the Parc Albert in Africa, from the Belgian government, to create a primate sanctuary, the land of gorillas that Dian Fossey would later visit.

In the early twentieth century, the diorama, like the cinema, replaced direct experience with a reproduction and, like the zoo, brought "back alive evidence of a world we could not otherwise know, now under apparent control" (Nichols 1988, p. 34). The diorama, Donna Haraway (1985b) suggests, gave nature a history; it offered itself as "a biography of nature," a realist production that was guided by the principles of organicism:

> The animals in the group form a developmental series, such that the group can represent the essence of the species as a dynamic, living whole. . . . There is no need for the multiplication of specimens because the series is a true biography. Each animal is an organism, and the group is an organism. Each organism is a vital moment in the narrative of natural history, condensing the flow of time into the harmony of developmental form. The groups are peaceful, composed, illuminated—in "brightest Africa." (p. 24)

A cross-coupling of organicism and realism, the diorama's truth was, however, based on its claim to reproduce the scientist's "original" experience in the "natural" setting.

Like other ethno-graphics, the diorama transfers the experience of the scientist to the viewer by transferring to the viewer an experience of visual detachment. The viewer is thus enabled to penetrate with his eye, meet the animal in nature without becoming nature, without becoming fully absorbed in the feminized spectacle.

> Nature is such a potent symbol of innocence partly because "she" is imagined to be without technology, to be the object of vision. . . . Man is not in nature partly because he is not seen, is not the spectacle. (Haraway 1985b, p. 52)

Participating in the diorama is, then, an initiation into manhood, constituting for the viewer one meaning of the masculine gender—"to be the unseen eye (I), the author" (p. 52).

The diorama suggests that scientific practices of transforming and transferring vision, constructed in the early decades of the twentieth century, were also part of a production of a colonial discourse, a racial fantasy of white male identity (Bhabha 1983), that transformed Africa from homeland to the site of the hunt, the location of research, the space of fieldwork. This transformation, visible in the diorama, served the scientist's identity and authority, as archaeologist Louis Leakey exemplifies when, in the opening scene of *Gorillas in the Mist,* he explains his presence in Africa and his research interest in the gorillas: "I want to know who I am and what it was that made me this way." In comparison with Leakey, Fossey's black guide is reduced to the stereotypical ethnographic informant, the colonized subject who is unable to become author, just as the officials of the local government, who turn their backs on gorilla poachers, seem unable to grasp the nobility of the apes, science, and the scientist's dispassionate commitment to research.

The "science of the naked eye," as Haraway describes empirical science, is not easily distinguished from the process of empire, a construction of racial and sexed identities. Indeed, it is these functions of empirical science, its disavowed strategies for textualizing local settings, that make its epistemology comforting. As it seemingly distinguishes fact and fiction, the image and the real, the observer and the observed, empiricism (con)serves the dominance of white masculinity, relating knowledge to man's personal and cultural enlightenment. But now, when these functions return to trouble empirical science, the science of the naked eye can only be fictionally retrieved, nostalgically represented in the figure of the woman.

Displacing this fiction of science is a science fiction in which the connection of science to acquiring knowledge as a form of enlightenment is undermined, if not mocked, as information-processing mechanisms dramatically demonstrate the "exteriority" of knowledge to the knower. With the proliferation of information-processing machines, Jean-François Lyotard (1984) argues,

> the relationship of the suppliers and users of knowledge to the knowledge they supply and use is now tending, and will increasingly tend, to assume the form already taken by the relationship of commodity producers and consumers to the commodities they produce and consume—that is, the

form of value. Knowledge is and will be produced in order to be sold, it is and will be consumed in order to be valorized in a new production: in both cases, the goal is exchange. Knowledge ceases to be an end in itself, it loses its "use-value." (pp. 4-5)

So, too, the truth of representation is no longer the question. Rather, the utility of the representation is what matters, as the machine interaction between users and suppliers is focused on ascertaining the meaning of a given situation, which the representation as simulation promotes rather than reflects. Thus, in *Alien*, it is through computer displays that the members of the *Nostromo*'s crew are informed as to where they are, how they are, and what the probabilities are that they will be in future situations. That is, it is computer technology that not only informs the crew but simulates the "natural" conditions that make it possible for the crew members to survive into the future. It is this utter dependency on the computer that elicits the sadomasochistic thematizations of computer use.

While in *Alien* the computer has been programmed to mislead the crew, leading to the annihilation of most of them, in *Aliens* this dangerous dependency is thematized in the way computer displays are used throughout the film to inform the crew (and viewers) of the whereabouts of the alien forms. The crew members become like elements in a computerized (war) game, as the film viewer is shown computerized information schematics that cue the imminent attack of a crew member by the alien as one dot representing the latter moves steadily toward another dot that represents the alien's soon-to-be victim. When both dots disappear from the computerized tracking device, the absence of information is the only representation of the loss of a crew member and the temporary quiescence of the alien. Toward the end of the film, as the last few crew members try to get away, they are shown crawling through a tunnellike space, chased by the alien forms, as if to reenact what the viewer has seen over and over again on computer displays.

The sadomasochistic pleasure of film viewing is conjoined with the painful pleasure of computer use, that is, with the fascination computer use offers in "the subordination of human volition to the operating constraints of the larger system" (Nichols 1988, p. 32). Although there is a sense of power in the control the computer offers the user, such control is granted only when the user has submitted to the passive position, to the preestablished constraints of the system. In *Alien*, the sadomasochistic pleasures of film viewing are extended seemingly without end, delivering the viewer to the pleasure of submitting to large, computerized systems, a submission that Ripley finally figures.

It would seem that in the context of computer technology, the narrative strategy of the naturalist machine produces heroines rather than heroes. In a final reduction of femininity to passivity, the woman can alternatively figure a romantic version of science's past or a domesticated version of a violent future for which science has become a primary source. Thus Ripley is victorious over the alien, but at the price of a complicated or desiring femininity. In the end, her femininity is fixed for her, simplified with the gaze of the camera. So, too, Dian Fossey becomes the fixed object of the camera, her life as much a spectacle as the gorillas are. Her life permits an overexposure of science's internal workings, a display of its rigors as riddled with repressed desires. For this she is killed, and a potentially feminist criticism of science is appropriated for a decadent reminiscence of science's "other times," when apes were apes and when to the white man it was clear that the woman and Africa were dark continents yet to be dominated and possessed.

The "terminator version" of realism, which Seltzer (1987) argues the naturalist novel presents, threatens to put an end to the realist project because in its perfect fit of body and machine, nature and artifice, it short-circuits the productive relays between what must, by necessity, appear as opposed. The significance of the heroine, I would propose, is to reinstate the project of realism in a cybernetic age of simulation. When, at the end of *Aliens,* Ripley returns home with the child and the man, and when, after her death, Dian Fossey talks in a voice-over about how she had expected to marry and have children instead of a mountain full of gorillas, these seem not only matters of narrative closure, putting the woman in her proper place. Given the heroics of these women, these final gestures seem more to keep the naturalist machine working, short of perfection. In finally having heroines seemingly represent themselves in images that reduce femininity to passivity, these heroines become subtle reminders of the fantasmatically repressed active feminine generativity, which can and will have its sequel in which to return, the enraged monstrosity of man's fantasy of a technology-out-of-control. Thus the oedipal logic is reenlisted for realist narrativity, in order to provide it with a mechanism of reducing difference to crude oppositions in the figures of masculinity and femininity.

REFERENCES

Bhabha, Homi. 1983. "The Other Question . . . ." *Screen* 24: 18-36.

Clover, Carol. 1987. "Her Body, Himself: Gender in the Slasher Film." *Representations* 20: 187-228.

Creed, Barbara. 1986. "Horror and the Monstrous-Feminine: An Imaginary Abjection." *Screen* 27: 44-70.

Dadoun, Roger. 1986. "*Metropolis*: Mother-City—'Mittler'—Hitler." *Camera Obscura* 15: 137-163.

Doane, Mary Ann. 1987. *The Desire to Desire.* Bloomington: Indiana University Press.

Ewen, Stuart. 1976. *Captains of Consciousness.* New York: McGraw-Hill.

Freud, Sigmund. 1962. *Three Essays on the Theory of Sexuality.* Translated by J. Stachey. New York: Basic Books.

Greenberg, Harvey. 1986. "Reimagining the Gargoyle: Psychoanalytic Notes on *Alien.*" *Camera Obscura* 15: 87-108.

Haraway, Donna. 1985a. "A Manifesto for Cyborgs." *Socialist Review* 80(March-April): 65-107.

————. 1985b. "Teddy Bear Patriarchy: Taxidermy in the Garden of Eden, New York City, 1908-1936." *Social Text* 11: 20-64.

Huyssen, Andreas. 1986. *After the Great Divide.* Bloomington: Indiana University Press.

Jardine, Alice. 1987. "Of Bodies and Technologies." In *Discussions in Contemporary Culture,* edited by Hal Foster. Seattle: Bay.

Lyotard, Jean-François. 1984. *The Postmodern Condition: A Report on Knowledge.* Translated by Geoff Bennington and Brian Massumi. Minneapolis: University of Minnesota Press.

Mulvey, Laura. 1975. "Visual Pleasure and Narrative Cinema." *Screen* 16: 6-18.

Nichols, Bill. 1988. "The Work of Culture in the Age of Cybernetic Systems." *Screen* 29: 22-47.

Penley, Constance. 1986. "Time Travel, Primal Scene, and the Critical Dystopia." *Camera Obscura* 15: 67-86.

Rogin, Michael. 1985. " 'The Sword Became a Flashing Vision': D. W. Griffith's 'The Birth of a Nation.' " *Representations* (Winter): 205-211.

Seltzer, Mark. 1986. "The Naturalist Machine." In *Sex, Politics, and Science in the Nineteenth-Century Novel,* edited by Ruth Bernard Yeazell. Baltimore: Johns Hopkins University Press.

————. 1987. "Statistical Persons." *Diacritics* 17(Fall): 82-98.

4

HOWARD S. BECKER
The Methodology of a Writing Observed

The very soul of Nature, writing is also the most flagrant artifice, as strategic
as it is spontaneous; and the mystery is then how writing can at once mirror
and manipulate experience, serve and rule it simultaneously. . . . Writing,
like women, marks a frontier between public and private, at once agonized
outpouring and prudent stratagem. (Eagleton [on Richardson's *Pamela*]
1982, pp. 45-46)

Responding to those feelings that sociologists say they have about themselves as writers—feelings that block their writing—Howard S. Becker
in *Writing for Social Scientists* (1986b) suggests the remedy of "freewriting," writing "whatever comes into your head, as fast as you can" (p. 54).
This Becker advises so that, in the end, sociological writing may clearly
reflect what is observed and concisely present what ordinary people are
actually doing (pp. 8, 95). Since a clear and concise writing style is only
part of what Becker considers to be good sociology, in *Writing for Social
Scientists* his own sociological writing style is folded back on itself,
making the sociologist visible as a writer. But this public revelation of

Author's Note: An earlier version of this chapter appeared as "Letters from Pamela:
Reading Howard S. Becker's *Writing for Social Scientists*," in *Symbolic Interaction,* Vol.
12, No. 1, pp. 159-170. Copyright 1989 by JAI Press, Inc. Used by permission of the
publisher.

the sociologist at the scene of writing is displaced as the scene of writing becomes a field site, a scene for observing others' writing practices. In *Writing for Social Scientists,* Becker takes the private, psychologically charged act of writing and treats what is troublesome about it "sociologically" (p. xi). Not only are the private troubles of writing shown to be a social problem, but the privacy of the writer is shown to be the primary source of the problem. Displaying social scientists' self-reported feelings of shame and frustration in writing, Becker constructs a sociological analysis of academic writing, blaming the social organization of academic writing for encouraging social scientists to write in isolation.

To address academic writing as a social problem, however, Becker must break through the isolation of the writer by urging him to reveal to others his "magical defenses" to maintain isolation (pp. 1-25). Thus the production of data by which a social problem is represented becomes at the same time the only treatment/solution of the problem. Becker thereby adjusts the cinematic realism with which Blumer's writings informed sociological discourse. The realism that Becker's writings propose is more about making public what seems to be private, a realism that makes sociology more like what Becker describes his classes on writing to be, that is, something resembling the "new California therapies," "which rely on people revealing their psyches or bodies in public and discovering that the revelation . . . does not kill" (p. 5).

In what follows, I want to argue that what *Writing for Social Scientists* makes clear is that Becker's emphasis on representing "ordinary people," or what he also refers to as "the plain folk," has shifted the focus of ethnographic discourse from an empiricism informed with a cinematic realism to an empiricism expressed through a realism characteristic of TV melodrama, which, following Ien Ang (1985), I will call "emotional realism" (p. 45). Emotional realism allows sociology to collapse the "inside" and the "outside," making sociological what is first described as psychological or private. It allows sociology to promote itself by eliciting a compulsive extroversion of interiority. Therefore, the clear and concise writing that Becker urges is not so much about the narrative construction of a totalizing viewpoint as it is about privileging the ordinary by bringing out in public(ation) the ordinariness of people's private lives—a melodrama of ordinary interiority.

While Becker has always focused his sociology on ordinary people, in his earlier writings he did so in order to champion the "underdog." These writings nonetheless elicited an ironic reading. They were criticized for

supporting "the well educated and highly placed bureaucratic official-
dom" and thereby creating for the post-World War II welfare state "the
first version of new Establishment sociology . . . a sociology compati-
ble with the new character of social reform in the United States" (Gouldner
1970, pp. 229, 238). I would propose that in Becker's more recent
writings, his concern for ordinary people by subjecting individual sensibility and self-feelings to sociological representation can also be read
ironically to align sociological discourse with what is often described
as characteristic of contemporary society: "greater supervision of subjects, decreased privacy yet increased withdrawal into a private family
world" (Abercrombie et al. 1986, p. 151). Emotional realism provides
a form of authority for sociological discourse at a time when observational methodology has already left its mark on society in the intensifi-
cation of self-surveillance.

Thus, in *Writing for Social Scientists,* Becker dismisses the author as
the sole producer of a text—not in the name of narrativity, as a poststructural, semiotic criticism does (Foucault 1970; Barthes 1977), but
in the name of the collective action of ordinary people. Becker (1982)
treats sociological writing as he does an "art work" that he argues is produced not by an author or individual genius, but by an "art world," that
is, "a network of people whose cooperative activity, organized via their
joint knowledge of conventional means of doing things, produces the
kind of art works that art world is noted for" (p. x).

Thus Becker rejects the possibility of fixing aesthetic value, but not
to open the text or work to a critical analysis of the ways it inscribes
practices of writing and reading or viewing. He borrows instead from
the "institutional approach" to aesthetics, in order to be done with aesthetics once and for all. He argues that the theorizing of aesthetic value only
legitimates what artists already are doing and just follows what distributing organizations and audiences already accept as art (pp. 145-153).
What Becker most likely finds appealing in this approach is its similar-
ity to his own "labeling theory" of deviance (Becker 1963). As the deviant
is one to whom the label has successfully been applied, so is art. As deviant behavior leads to the construction of deviant motivation, so the
artwork leads to aesthetic evaluation, and not the other way around. If
Becker argues that "doing" precedes the definition or meaning of what
is done, it is only to evidence the social or collective action of what is
seemingly privatized, individual, or psychological.

Becker's rejection of the author, the artistic genius, or the delinquent
personality derives not only from his understanding of sociology as the

direct examination (participant observation) of what ordinary people are "actually doing," and therefore, "to decide theoretical problems empirically" (1986b, p. 95). It also derives from his understanding of sociology as a representational form that should foreground the value of ordinary people in a society overwhelmed by systems. Thus Becker argues that the sociologist understands only what "many people are already pretty much aware of" (1982, p. x), but that the sociologist's understanding is "deeper," because he "took the trouble to be there" and "see it" (1986b, pp. 36-37). Yet, what the sociologist sees is that the people he observes already "see" sociologically. As Becker explains, while people "still want to know 'why he did it' and still look for explanations of behavior in internalized values or inner compulsions . . . , [they] simultaneously use explanations based in society" (1986a, p. 1). People, Becker reports, "see the workings of 'systems' everywhere from the eco-system to the family" (p. 1).

What is left for the sociologist to make visible is "people doing things together" and in a way that arouses self-feeling in the face of the anonymity of large systems. If the concise and clear writing style Becker urges is meant to give a sense of reality, it is not through the construction of a totalizing viewpoint but with the emotional tones that representing ordinary lives evokes. Indeed, for Becker, sociology produces factual representations when it evokes self-feeling, when it makes plain that society is no more than the collective action of ordinary people (1986b, pp. 82-102; see also 1986a, p. 9). Thus Becker informs sociological discourse with an emotional realism by reshaping ethnography, focusing on the relationship of participant observation and the life history method.

In what follows, I want to discuss emotional realism as a development of the realisms that I have already begun to describe, suggesting that Becker gives sociological discourse a form of authority that draws on the melodramatic form of television but also on a history of the relationship of a clear and concise writing style to the life history, the autobiography, and the realist novel. This history conditions the institutionalization of the opposition of factual and fictional discourses in terms of which melodrama becomes a vehicle of signifying emotion, especially in television. Then, in a rereading of a chapter in *Writing for Social Scientists* written by Pamela Richards, I suggest how the woman writer is made to figure a new writing technology for sociological discourse.

SOCIOLOGICAL DISCOURSE
AND PLAIN STYLE

When Becker first argued for the centrality of the life history to socio-logical discourse and methodology, he did so by comparing the life history to the novel and the autobiography. Like the novel, Becker (1970) argues, the life history has "dramatic urgency" but is more concerned than the novel "with the faithful rendering of the subject's experience" (p. 64). Like the autobiography, life history has a "first person point of view" but it is not a partial or self-interested story as autobiography is (p. 64). Thus, by assuming the opposition of factual and fictional discourses, Becker distinguishes the life history as an empirical scientific method-ology, central to sociological discourse.

But, as I have already suggested and as even Becker's remarks imply, the distinction of sociological discourse from the novel and the autobi-ography is a problematic one, since the ethnography informs sociolog-ical discourse with an oedipal logic of narrativity that authorizes factual representation through a reconstruction of a subject's struggle for iden-tity or what might be described as a life history. What is lost in Becker's description of the life history is how its form historically developed in relationship to both a clear and concise writing style and the opposition of factual and fictional discourses.

Such a history might begin, as Lennard Davis (1983) suggests, at the end of the Renaissance, with the first "news ballads," then also called novels. The ballad was the first printed prose narrative that was meant to be read to those who would listen, rather than a tale just spoken aloud. It "reported" events shortly after their occurrence, or at least it was made to seem so. What gave the ballads the appearance of "newsworthi-ness" was that they were offered as first-person, self-disclosed accounts of events. But since the first person of the ballad was a fiction, it was a fictional self-disclosure that made newness, true or factual. This fic-tional construction of facticity worked, Davis argues, because it seem-ingly allowed the reader to see events as they actually happened.

Indeed, the oft-repeated illustration that accompanied the ballad was "the crost couple of good misfortune," in which a man and a woman making love are overseen by the narrator/reader, the latter figured as a disembodied head in the background in the illustration:

> The significant fact is that the reader is seen both as a primary subject within
> the ballad as well as the voyeur outside the frame of the ballad. . . . the

reader's functions are split in a way I would think was unique to this discourse—that is, the reader is at once subject and object. . . . ballads can preach at readers to obey various religious and moral precepts and at the same time permit those same readers to voyeuristically watch these transgressions as they are described. (Davis 1983, p. 61)

The illustration of the "crost couple" points not only to the ballad's eroticization of reading and writing, but also to its emphasis on a "visual epistemology," which based knowledge on seeing. Both of these characteristics, as I have already argued, were central in the development of realism in the eighteenth century. But their relationship to a clear and concise writing style refers back to the seventeenth century, when language was perceived to need safeguards against its own potential to be used ideologically, as it was in the English revolution. The Puritan "plain style" was offered as a corrective, providing for truth by intertwining "protestant belief . . . with the evidence of the senses" (McKeon 1987, p. 76).

Thus plain style was not so much a figurative-free writing as a writing rich in "reference to the plain things of this world" (p. 76). The plain things of everyday life were presented so that the reader could "see" the spirituality embedded in their very ordinariness. Eventually, the accounting of an ordinary life would become a primary way to show God's providential plan and later to illuminate the overarching pattern of human history. Thus the life history as it came to inform the autobiography and later the novel, but also social science and history, embedded an orientation that was not merely that of the individual writer or subject. The unfolding character of the subject not only constituted the story of his everyday life, but at the same time gave evidence, seemingly visible evidence, to an overarching pattern or historicity. In the life history, a clear and concise writing style or the plain style became characterized by an intermixture of historicity and sense evidence and thereby became the "truthful" form of self-disclosure, the form of factuality that would finally necessitate the opposition of fictional and factual discourses.

Thus factual and fictional discourses were increasingly institutionalized as opposed discourses because the life history was no longer taken to be only autobiographical, that is, to be about an actual person. It had become a narrative form.

When the first person experiencer, narrator and hero, was appropriated from autobiography for the sake of "realism" in the new, bourgeois novel, the presence of such a narrator was no longer enough to distinguish autobiography. . . . When the formal delights of direct observation, eyewitness testimony, and density of domestic detail became more general literary phenomena, they no longer appeared distinctively autobiographical. (Bruss 1976, p. 9)

Davis (1983, pp. 193-211) argues that the novel became distinctly fictional when Fielding fitted an invented life history to a reconstruction of actual political events without disclaiming the fictionality of the life history. In novels such as Richardson's *Pamela,* the author claimed only to be editing factual material—in the case of *Pamela,* letters written by an actual servant girl. But with Fielding, the novel is no longer claimed to be true because it reports what happened to an actual person. It claimed instead to be realistic.

In the novel, the life history became the productive form of a realist history or story of society and culture. The realist novel consolidated a general form of reading and writing that would permit plain style to operate in either factual or fictional discourses, as a signification of reality. Privatizing the public and making the private public (or publishable), the novel taught readers and writers a form of knowing that "sees into" a character's development in order to "see out" to history, society, and culture. Plain style, therefore, asserted the interiority of the subject and the privacy of the domestic sphere as these were nonetheless adjusted to the public sphere, as published facts of empirical reality.

Indeed, Richardson's *Pamela* was a privileged text in relationship to the development of the public sphere. As Terry Eagleton (1982) describes it, "Pamela was less a 'novel,' than a password or badge of allegiance, code for what became in effect a whole event" (p. 5). It educated the reader in a new sensibility, the new civility of ordinary language. Plain style became a hallmark of the artfulness of ordinary virtue or true identity, allowing for a displacement of an aristocratic culture with a "middle-class" one.

> The eighteenth century middle class must do more than amass capital or trade in titles. Its moral power (which Pamela is made to represent) must permeate the texture of civil society, pitting the values of thrift, peace and chastity against a violent and profligate nobility. (p. 6)

In her letters and journal entries, Pamela is made by Richardson to bemoan the sexual aggressions of her master/employer, who eventually becomes her husband. Pamela's writings are stolen by her master and thus readers read how he secretly reads what she has secretly written of his sexual assertions. Pamela insists on "a radical constancy to internals —to love over convenience, to virtue over birth, fortune and honor" (McKeon 1987, p. 372). Her aristocratic master's

> ultimately successful struggle to conceive it, all the same, is inseparable both from the irresistible force of his love for Pamela and from the triumph of her notion of "honor" over his. And these circumstances, in turn, depend entirely on the power of Pamela's mind, on her extraordinary capacity to create a utopian projection of possibility while she is ostensibly and passively contained by the limiting boundaries of domestic service and domestic incarceration at the Linconshire estate. (pp. 372-373)

Thus the sentiments of the feminized, domestic sphere were transposed onto civil society and were exploited in the fashioning of the new ideological formation of the bourgeois public sphere. This transposition changed the private sphere as well: The constraints of patriarchy were loosened, thus permitting the publication of the private world. Thus the novel produced a privatized form of knowing that connected factuality to the exposure of self-feelings or self-revelations. This form of knowing placed such demands on the subject's interiority that eventually the overexposure of the private world would require an excess in representation to evoke emotion at all.

It is this excess that has come to characterize the emotional realism of television as it exploits the exposure of the subject's interiority to near collapse. Thus, in television, the opposition of private and public as well the opposition of factual and fictional discourses fades as the exposure of the private world can no longer signify reality as history or a story of society and culture. Self-revelation becomes compulsive without end, without the end of envisioning a reality external to the image.

THE TELEVISUAL
AND EMOTIONAL REALISM

While in the realisms of the novel and narrative cinema it is the production of a factual knowledge of reality that matters, in emotional realism what matters is "a subjective experience of the world: a 'structure of feeling.' It is emotions which count in a structure of feeling"

(Ang 1985, p. 45). Rather than eliciting the viewer's unconscious identifications, emotional realism affects the viewer's feelings by focusing the viewer on an experience of self, without necessarily referencing a historical or social reality. This focus on self-feelings, Ang argues, is central to a melodramatic imagination or the "tragic structure of feeling" of TV soap-operatic form (pp. 41-46).

If in the melodramatic imagination no historical or social reality is represented through the presentation of the private, it is because the private events presented are not those of a character's subject development, the unity of which informs representations of history and society. Rather, melodrama operates on what Thomas Elsaesser (1972) describes as a "non-psychological conception of the *dramatis personae,* who figure less as autonomous individuals than to transmit the action and link the various locales within a total constellation" (p. 2). Rather than the drama being within the subject, it is between the figures, which function in situations only to display excessively the ups and downs of ordinary, everyday life.

Thus it is argued that the emotional realism or the melodrama of television soap operas increasingly characterizes all TV programming. As Lawrence Grossberg (1987) puts it, "TV's most powerful annunciation is its emotionalism, the fact that it is structured by a series of movements between extreme highs and extreme lows" (p. 43). The extension of the soap-operative or melodramatic form throughout TV programming may even mark what Mark Crispin Miller (1986) describes as "the maturing of the media." As TV comes into its own, reality is colonized in rather than represented by its images.

> How, then, has TV "matured"? Certainly, it has fulfilled none of its documentary or dramatic possibilities, a failure that explains the character of TV's recent consummation. For in order to "bring you the world," whether through reportage or drama, TV would have to point beyond itself. Yet "the maturing of the medium" consists precisely in TV's near-perfect inability to make any such outward gesture. TV tends now to bring us nothing but TV. . . . TV now exalts TV spectatorship by preserving a hermetic vision that is uniformly televisual. . . . TV has almost purified itself, aspiring to a spectacle that can remind us of no prior or extrinsic vision. (pp. 193-194)

TV makes visible the breakdown of the opposition of the real and the image. As Lynne Joyrich (1988) describes it, "the territory of the real is no longer mapped onto a representation, but the map precedes the territory—events are already inscribed by the media in advance as television is diffracted into reality and the real is diffracted into TV" (p. 137). At the same time, TV stages "hysterical attempts to find stakes of meaning," with a nostalgia for "signs of reality, tradition, and lived experience" (p. 137). Emotional realism and melodrama thereby displace and defuse the anxiety that TV provokes, over the breakdown of the opposition of reality and image by enacting the moral struggle of ordinary life and insisting on the irreducibility of its essential truth. As Ang (1985) argues:

> The melodramatic imagination is therefore the expression of a refusal, or inability, to accept insignificant everyday life as banal and meaningless, and is born of a vague, inarticulate dissatisfaction with existence here and now. . . . There are no words for the ordinary pain of living of ordinary people in the modern welfare state, for the vague sense of loss, except in half-ironic, half-resigned phrases such as: "You win some, you lose some." By making that ordinariness something special and meaningful in the imagination, that sense of loss can—at least for a time—be removed. (pp. 79 80)

Staging moral struggle only in terms of private, ordinary, everyday life, TV melodrama is both a function of and a mechanism for the increasing privatization of the public. By making ordinariness special and by evoking a specifically private form of moral struggle, TV melodrama repeats, albeit nostalgically or cynically, what first characterized the melodrama in the eighteenth century, that is, its "radically democratic, striving to make its representations clear and legible to everyone" (Brooks 1976, p. 15). Melodrama thereby embeds a desire for a "clear, unambiguous and impressive" language, a language signifying more fully as if with natural gestures or cries, a language anyone could understand (pp. 67-68). In a sense, melodrama embeds a desire for no language at all, what Mary Ann Doane (1987, pp. 84-85) describes as a fantasmatic return to the pre-oedipal maternal space, before the subject is structured by language, structured in sexual difference. Thus melodrama speaks an uneasiness about language, about language's capacity to be expressive enough, to express enough of ordinary life. Melodrama also focuses on figures who can be looked at, who are lacking in power and whose moral struggle therefore is seemingly apparent.

EMOTIONAL REALISM IN THE
FIGURE OF THE WOMAN WRITER

The clear and concise writing style that Becker proposes for socio-logical discourse has a political history, connecting it through the figure of the underdog or ordinary person, to the rise of the bourgeois public sphere and its demise, to the realism of the novel and the melodrama of television, to the privatization of virtue in the domestic sphere and the reconstruction of the family as the locus of mass consumption. And if Becker's earlier writings prepared sociological discourse for the appro-priation of the emotional realism of television, his more recent writings on representation itself even promote, as television does, the blurring of genres and discourses. Indeed, in his study of the ways of "telling about society," Becker (1986a) includes the following for analysis:

> From the social sciences, such modes of representation as mathematical models, statistical tables and graphs, maps, ethnographic prose, and histor-ical narrative; from the arts, novels, films, still photographs, and drama; from the large shadowy area in between, life histories and other biograph-ical and autobiographical materials, reportage (including the mixed genres of docudrama, documentary film, and fictionalized fact), and the storytell-ing, mapmaking, and other representation activities of lay people (or people acting in a lay capacity, as even professionals do most of the time). (pp. 122-123)

While there is yet something of a distinction between art and social science, that distinction is not about the "faithfulness of the rendition," as it had been when Becker first distinguished the life history from the autobiography and the novel. Indeed, the life history is characterized now as being "from the large shadowy area in between" science and art. Now, Becker argues that it is the use to which the representation is put that matters:

> It seems more useful, more likely to lead to new understanding, to think of every way of representing social reality as *perfect*—for something. The question is what it is good for. The answer to that is organizational. Despite the superficial differences between genres and media, the same fundamen-tal problems occur in every medium. (p. 125)

While still insisting that good sociology is to be written in a clear and concise style, Becker nonetheless gives shape to a realism that no longer needs to oppose fact and fiction, private and public. There is even something of an envious idealization of artworks, the effectiveness of which no longer raises the question of faithfulness or veridicality for anyone. Commenting on the photographs of Hans Haacke, Becker proposes:

> Haacke, operating in an art world with methods and results in many ways similar to those of social scientist, gets very different and much more substantial reactions to his work than social scientists get, in their world, to their work. His work provokes reactions from relevant parties. . . . Haacke's work has the appearance of unquestioned validity because the customary response of the art world to works of art no longer includes the possibility of questioning the veridicality of the statement the work makes. . . . the question of faithfulness is no longer of interest to anyone . . . it is enough that the image be formally interesting or emotionally compelling. (p. 115)

In Becker's writings, increasingly sociological discourse is also expected to be formally interesting or emotionally compelling. It is to be good for the representation of ordinary people.

It would seem, then, that for Becker, sociology is not only to be about ordinary people but to be for them, a seemingly democratic sociology that provides representation for anyone and everyone. But, like the melodramatic form they urge, Becker's writings are ambiguously radical. They situate sociological discourse somewhere between a politically self-conscious form of representation and a form of escapism, engulfing the reader and writer in a nostalgia for the absence of conflict and difference.

If I would argue that Becker's writings are more nostalgic than critical, it is because they become complicit with an erasure of the politics of sexuality that makes possible the publication of the private and the privatization of the public as a guise for democracy. Thus, in *Writing for Social Scientists,* Becker's disavowal of the political history of a clear and concise writing style is also a disavowal of the relationship of reading and writing to the oedipal logic of sexual difference. But this logic returns to trouble Becker's text in the chapter by Pamela Richards, which is written in the form of a letter to Becker. The chapter is an autobiographical response to the question Becker poses to Richards as to why she feels that writing is, as she describes it, "a very high-risk operation" (p. 110). Thus this chapter makes a place for a woman but also marks her double displacement as a figure. As her self-analysis is enclosed in the man's text, she becomes the data of his analysis, the figure of the subject that the text constructs.

Actually, there are two autobiographical chapters in *Writing for Social Scientists*. The first is Becker's self-asserting chapter, which is a step-by-step progression to his success as a writer. The second is Pamela Richards's; it tells of her becoming a writer, but her progress is haunted by her fear of being a fraud:

> I am a fraud because I don't work the way everyone else does. I don't read anything except weird novels and stuff that has nothing to do with my "work." I don't sit in the library taking notes; I don't read the journals cover to cover; and what's worse, I don't want to. I am not a scholar. I am not a sociologist because I don't know any sociology. I haven't the commitment to steep myself in the ideas and thoughts of The Masters. I couldn't converse meaningfully about The Literature on any topic including those in which I am allegedly a specialist. Even worse, I have the temerity to claim that I am doing a study of women's prisons, when in fact I haven't done it right. (in Becker 1986b, pp. 112-113)

The figure of the fraudulent woman fractures Richards's chapter in two. In the first part, her thoughts about writing about her study of imprisoned women compel her to report her dreams: "I just finished two cups of coffee while thinking about the issue of risk. My meditations have to start with three dreams that I've had in the last week" (p. 11). The second part is Richards's interpretation of her dreams, which she uses to encourage herself to take the risk of writing: "If I actually write something down, I'm liable to win a bit and lose a bit" (p. 120). I want to give another reading of Richards's dreams, of their placement in a chapter of Becker's text. I will treat the figure of "the woman coming to writing" for the way it mirrors to the man an image of himself as a successful writer/writing teacher. I read the reinscription of Richards's dreams in Becker's text as making her more a character than an author, more a figure of the text's enunciation.

Becker thereby draws on the feminine figure to articulate the structure of feeling that is proposed by his text. He draws her as the figure of the subject of late capitalist society, the self-revealing, self-accounting subject. Just as the letters of Richardson's *Pamela* provided an exemplary expression of the value of bourgeois society, Pamela Richards's letter enacts the structure of feeling that Becker's text proposes for sociological discourse. Her letter is the private within the public discourse—a privacy that is publicized, a feeling tone that is exteriorized.

In Richardson's *Pamela,* the risks for a woman writer are expressed by the male author who is masquerading as a woman. Thus Richardson has Pamela write how her master, when he finds out how she has hidden her paper, pens, and letters in her undergarments, threatens to undress her to get at her writing. The metaphor of male penetration for the author's assertion is put in place, as the woman's passive position becomes the metaphor for the blank page on which the author writes (Showalter 1982, pp. 9-35; Gubar 1982). These metaphors give the lie to the claim that Pamela authored the book of letters that Richardson professes only to have edited. Making the woman figure the male author can also make explicit the inconsistency between the bourgeois ideal of a public discourse open to everyone and women's actual struggles to become self-authored. Thus when Richardson has Pamela's master hold her captive in the woods, it makes visible the mental captivity women struggled against in order to write. This struggle is with the figurative penning in by men.

How, then, could Pamela Richards write up her study of imprisoned women without herself struggling against those versions of women penned in by men? Thus Richards writes "from a cabin in the woods," where she has secluded herself in order to experiment with "freewriting," but which leads instead to her writing about her fraudulence and her dreams. In the first dream, Richards's written work is brutally criticized by a woman friend and colleague. To Richards, it was as if her colleague "wanted to take me by the shoulders and shake me till my teeth fell out" (p. 111). In the second dream, Richards is not writing but speaking about her study, and she feels "very powerful and fully in command of what I was doing" (p. 112). Richards then reports that she had been reading Lillian Hellman's *An Unfinished Woman* and *Pentimento.* "Over and over and over. I don't quite know why" (p. 112). In the second dream, when Richards spoke, what she said seemed "as if Lillian Hellman were writing it—it was exactly the same style, the same marching sentences, the same feel and expression" (p. 112). And there is the third dream that is finally claimed not to be an actual dream but rather "a different sort of midnight event," from which Richards awoke with a "crystalline conviction: I knew absolutely and with complete certainty, that I was a fraud" (p. 112). This knowledge, Richards claims, "wasn't constructed through some explicit argument; it didn't develop out of anything I recognized; it was just there" (p. 112).

As if to echo Freud's (1962, p. 61) claim that the girl knows her fraudulence immediately at the sight of the boy's penis, which she lacks,

Richards feels she can fake authority only when she uses the pen. No longer able to identify with the woman author, she identifies instead with the female spectator, who is stereotyped as being wrapped in the image, lost to it (Doane 1987, pp. 12-13). Thus she presents herself not as a writer but as a reader and "not of The Masters" but of "weird" novels and autobiographies, "stuff that has nothing to do with my 'work'." (p. 112).

Here is the woman writer searching for an identity against the versions of women provided by male-inscribed texts: convicted to the crystalline mirror of the wicked Queen Mother or the crystalline coffin of the virginal Snow White. Thus the wicked mother/woman friend/colleague betrays Richards as if pulling out her teeth, castrating her, taking away her bite. She is the jealous mother who delivers the male's sentencing of women to the mirror, to being the man's image.

The Queen Mother is a witch, an energetic schemer. Caught in the looking glass with no outer prospects, the Queen plots or makes stories and, as Sandra Gilbert and Susan Gubar (1979, pp. 38-39) point out, Snow White, although docile and sweetly domestic, is nonetheless responsive to these plots as she is tempted by the Queen's offers of a comb, an apple, and lace stays. Gilbert and Gubar conclude: "The Queen and Snow White are in some sense one: while the Queen struggles to free herself from the passive Snow White in herself, Snow White must struggle to repress the assertive Queen in herself" (p. 41).

For the woman coming to writing, the struggle is in part against the actual exclusion from the pen, usually dramatized as a struggle against dominant institutions. It is also the struggle against the internalized characterizations of the woman, dramatized as a struggle over phallicity. Indeed, by the nineteenth century, the characterization of the woman as either angel or monster had come to shape the political unconscious of Western women, informing their textual productions (Gilbert and Gubar 1979).

Described as the "embodiment of just those extremes of mysterious and intransigent Otherness" (Gilbert and Gubar 1979, p. 19), the woman's choice seemed to be between parts of herself; either she could be a woman or she could write. And if she did write, her experience of writing was often felt as a suffering in and of the body that itself had become like a glass coffin (Gubar 1982, pp. 73-93). Thus, in order to write, the woman of that century looked for herself with "a searching glance into the mirror of the male-inscribed text," finding there, on the other side of the mirror, "an enraged prisoner: herself" (Gilbert and Gubar 1979, p. 15).

For a woman to write as a woman, she must write self-productively—
that is, autobiographically—so as to create herself as a writer as she
writes. But she must also deconstruct the oedipal logic of realist narrativity that allows authority only in the disavowal of sexual difference.
Without the deconstructive approach, a woman writer can reproduce, as
Hellman does, what needs to be worked through. Thus although Hellman's
writing is a search for a woman writer's identity, it leaves her in the end
"an unfinished woman." Hellman creates the pentimento or layers of
persona against which she wants to see herself, and finally she settles
on Bethe as her model. Bethe, the unrelated wonderer, never mother,
never wife, but sexual lover, gives Hellman the permission to live openly
with Hammett (Demetrakopoulos 1980; Billson and Smith 1980). In
Hammett, Hellman finds an unfaithful man, like her father, but one who
seemingly can protect her from the jealous mother. As the "cool teacher
who would not be impressed or disturbed by a strange and difficult girl"
(Hellman 1969, p. 44), Hammett is Hellman's choice and thus she can
be a writer, with pen but without husband and children—a writer and
an unfinished woman. Not that being a woman is a matter of "having it
all"; what matters is the unconscious fantasy installed as the mechanism
for a woman's writing. What is the unconscious fantasy that Richards
elicits for herself and the reader when she imagines herself writing and
thus "to win a bit and lose a bit" (in Becker 1986b, p. 120)?

What Richardson would have Pamela do, for actual women to do, has
been and is a political and psychic struggle. Therefore, I have reread
Richards's dreams misprisioning them from their being an inscription
of the male author. I have reread them as part of a history of women's
dreams and fears, especially remembering that other Pamela who seemingly won her battle "for self-preservation and self-advancement" by
changing her master's understanding of words (Spacks 1976, p. 210).
Thus, while Richardson (mis)used the figure of the woman as a way of
"constructing and impressing his class's new morality, language, eti-
quette, even literary forms upon British culture," women did not only
identify Pamela as a "male-constructed symbol of bourgeois individualism (ultimately empowered through words)"; they also read Pamela
as a symbol "of women's powerlessness" (Smith-Rosenberg 1987, pp. 24-
25). Women reread Richardson's displacements onto the woman in terms
of their own fantasies and dreams. It is with rereadings that women
textualize their fierce struggle with authorship, leaving traces of desire.

When Becker (1970, p. 123) first championed a sociology sensitive to
ordinary people, he nevertheless insisted on a sentiment-free sociology.

He urged a sociology that is free from the distortions of sympathy. He complained then that methodology textbooks fail us. They tell us how to avoid error but not how to use "all safeguards available to us" to defend against the distortions of sympathy (p. 132). With *Writing for Social Scientists,* Becker provides the needed textbook. Yet its message is not so much about methods of sociological research as it is about methods of sociological writing. Shifting from a methodological context to the context of writing, Becker can be reread to suggest that writing is the site for managing sentiment and sympathy by negotiating the reader's or writer's emotional relationship to himself through regulating his relationship to the text.

Thus Becker's demand for a clear and concise writing is a demand for a writing that evokes a certain sentiment, a certain sympathy, even while appearing to be sentiment-free. Defending himself against sentimentality while informing sociological discourse with an emotional realism, Becker uses the figure of the woman writer to embody those sentiments the sociologist can then appear only to give expression:

> I beg you will write a few Lines to them and let me prescribe the Form for it; which I have done, putting myself as near as I can in your Place, and expressing your Sense, with a Warmth that I doubt will have too much possess'd you. (Her master to Pamela about her letter writing; Richardson 1971, p. 108)

REFERENCES

Abercrombie, Nicholas et al. 1986. *Sovereign Individuals of Capitalism.* London: Allen & Unwin.

Ang, Ien. 1985. *Watching Dallas.* New York: Hill & Wang.

Barthes, Roland. 1977. *Image-Music-Text.* Translated by Stephen Heath. New York: Hill & Wang.

Becker, Howard S. 1963. *Outsider.* New York: Free Press.

———. 1970. *Sociological Work.* New Brunswick, NJ: Transaction.

———. 1982. *Art Worlds.* Berkeley: University of California Press.

———. 1986a. *Doing Things Together.* Evanston, IL: Northwestern University Press.

———. 1986b. *Writing for Social Scientists.* Chicago: University of Chicago Press.

Billson, Marcus and Sidonia Smith. 1980. "Lillian Hellman and the Strategy of the Other." In *Women's Autobiography,* edited by Estelle C. Jelinck. Bloomington: Indiana University Press.

Brooks, Peter. 1976. *The Melodramatic Imagination: Balzac, Henry James, Melodrama, and the Mode of Excess.* New Haven, CT: Yale University Press.

Bruss, Elizabeth. 1976. *Autobiographical Acts: The Changing Situation of a Literary Genre.* Baltimore: Johns Hopkins University Press.

Davis, Lennard. 1983. *Factual Fictions: The Origins of the English Novel.* New York: Columbia University Press.

Demetrakopoulos, Stephanie. 1980. "The Metaphysics of Matrilinearism in Women's Autobiography." In *Women's Autobiography,* edited by Estelle C. Jelinck. Bloomington: Indiana University Press.

Doane, Mary Ann. 1987. *The Desire to Desire.* Bloomington: Indiana University Press.

Eagleton, Terry. 1982. *The Rape of Clarissa.* Minneapolis: University of Minnesota Press.

Elsaesser, Thomas. 1972. "Tales of Sound and Fury: Observations on the Family Melodrama." *Monogram* 4: 2-15.

Foucault, Michel. 1970. *The Order of Things.* New York: Pantheon.

Freud, Sigmund. 1962. *Three Essays on the Theory of Sexuality.* Translated by R. Hurley. New York: Vintage.

Gilbert, Sandra and Susan Gubar. 1979. *The Madwoman in the Attic.* New Haven, CT: Yale University Press.

Gouldner, Alvin. 1970. "The Sociologist as Partisan: Sociology and the Welfare State." In *The Sociology of Sociology,* edited by Larry Reynolds and Janice Reynolds. New York: David McKay.

Grossberg, Lawrence. 1987. "The In-Difference of Television." *Screen* 28: 28-45.

Gubar, Susan. 1982. " 'The Blank Page' and the Issues of Female Creativity." In *Writing and Sexual Difference,* edited by Elizabeth Abel. Chicago: University of Chicago Press.

Hellman, Lillian. 1969. *An Unfinished Woman.* New York: Bantam.

Joyrich, Lynne. 1988. "All That Television Allows: TV Melodrama, Postmodernism and Consumer Culture." *Camera Obscura* 16: 129-153.

McKeon, Michael. 1987. *The Origins of the English Novel 1600-1740.* Baltimore: Johns Hopkins University Press.

Miller, Mark Crispin. 1986. "Deride and Conquer." In *Watching Television,* edited by Todd Gitlin. New York: Pantheon.

Richardson, Samuel. 1971. *Pamela.* Boston: Houghton Mifflin.

Seltzer, Mark. 1984. "Reading Foucault: Cells, Corridors, Novels." *Diacritics* (Spring): 78-89.

Showalter, Elaine. 1982. "Feminist Criticism in the Wilderness." In *Writing and Sexual Difference,* edited by Elizabeth Abel. Chicago: University of Chicago Press.

Smith-Rosenberg, Carroll. 1987. "Misprisioning Pamela: Representations of Gender and Class in Nineteenth-Century America." *Michigan Quarterly Review* 26: 9-28.

Spacks, Patricia. 1976. *Imagining a Self.* Cambridge, MA: Harvard University Press.

5

STEVEN SPIELBERG'S
PRODUCTION OF THE
MINIATURIZATION OF MAN

> Desire, authority, you examine that, and you are led right back—to the father. You can even fail to notice that there's no place at all for women in the operation! In the extreme the world of "being" can function to the exclusion of the mother. No need for mother—provided that there is something of the maternal: and it is the father then who acts as—is—the mother. Either the woman is passive; or she doesn't exist. What is left is unthinkable, unthought of. She does not enter into the oppositions, she is not coupled with the father (who is coupled with the son). (Cixous 1980, pp. 91-92)

In a review of films of the late 1960s through early 1980s such as *Poltergeist, Rosemary's Baby, Ordinary People, ET, Starman, Shoot the Moon, Back to the Future, Carrie, The Exorcist, The Amityville Horror,* and *Close Encounters of the Third Kind,* Vivian Sobchack (1986) suggests that there was a convergence of cultural meanings that the figures of the father and the child thematized across three genres of film—the horror film, the science fiction film, and the family melodrama film. The generic exchange of figures and themes, Sobchack argues, allowed for the dramatization of "the crisis experienced by American bourgeois patriarchy since the late 1960's, and the related disintegration and transfiguration of the 'traditional' American bourgeois family" (pp. 7-8). In these film productions, bureaucratic structures such as the government, the military, and the multinational corporation are often treated critically. But so too is the family. The father disaffected with bureaucracy returns home, so to speak, only to find the family to be but another, if not the "real," source of his alienation.

If the horror film, which makes the home its favored site, shows the father as the subject or object of "a desire for the annihilation of patriarchy" (p. 14), the family melodrama, which explores family disintegration, shows fathers as "powerless, harmless . . . little more than children themselves" (p. 15). Thus the father appears either as a grotesque figure or as an impotent one, while the child is figured either as evil but powerful or vulnerable but prescient, if not parental. But neither the family melodrama nor the horror film represents a successful solution to the crisis of patriarchy:

> If the child is figured as powerful at the "expense" of the Father, then patriarchy is threatened; if Father is figured as powerful at the "expense" of his child, then paternity is threatened. In both cases, the traditional and conceivable future is threatened—for if patriarchy is willfully destroyed by its children, no "tradition" will mark the future with the past and present, and if paternity is willfully denied by a patriarchy which destroys its children, then the future will not be "conceived." (p. 17)

Where the horror film and the family melodrama fail, the science fiction film, Sobchack argues, succeeds as a conservative resolution of the crisis of patriarchy or what might also be described as a challenge to the oedipal logic of realist narrativity in relationship to the masculine figure, changes in technology, and political economic arrangements. If, then, the science fiction film focuses on the disintegration of the family, it does so in order to "liberate" paternity from familial relationships. Oedipality is seemingly denied, as the staging of the male's quest is situated elsewhere; in the fantasmatic time-space of extraterrestriality, the value of paternity can be rearticulated along with male domination.

In this chapter, I want to offer a rereading of Steven Spielberg's productions of science fiction in order to argue that these films narrativize the denigration of the father's authority within the family. Spielberg's productions thereby enact a fantasmatic regression to pre-oedipality in order to disavow oedipality altogether. Collapsing the figure of the father with the figure of the child, these films allow a reconfiguration of the masculine subject. Masculinity situates itself in the place of the mother; it appropriates the mother's place for what I would describe as the male-mothering systems of the state. In doing so, Spielberg's science fiction also manages the dismantling of cinematic realism and the coming to dominance of the televisual. Spielberg's science fiction transforms the movie viewer into a television watcher, finally saving the oedipal logic of realist narrativity.

THE MEDIA PRODUCTION
OF THE FATHER

If in films of the late 1960s through early 1980s the father was often figured as grotesque or impotent, Mark Crispin Miller (1986) notes that the father was also a ridiculed figure in the television situation comedies of the same period. On television, Dad is often made the butt of some domestic joke, a joke enjoyed by those who are supposedly more at home in the home: the kids and their mother.

In prime time, Dad is not the only one who is presented as foolish and incompetent, however. Eventually, each and every family member is ridiculed by some other member. What might at first appear as a "comic blow" against Dad (Miller 1986, p. 206) in the name of women and children instead turns out to be "ridicule of all by all," "the very essence of the modern sitcom" (p. 214). Seemingly just one member of a community of underlings, the TV dad never fully hides his "intimidating hardness," his "uncompromising willfulness," which makes him just the right character for corporate advertising (pp. 210-211). Taking Bill Cosby as an example of a TV dad, Miller argues:

> At once solicitous and overbearing, he personifies the corporate force that owns him. Like it, he comes across as an easygoing parent, and yet, also like it, he cannot help but betray the impulse to coerce. We see that he is bigger than we are, better known, better off, and far more powerfully sponsored. Thus, we find ourselves ambiguously courted, just like those tots who eat up lots of Jell-O pudding under his playful supervision. (p. 211)

Thus Miller suggests a relationship between the denigration of the father's authority and the maturation of the televisual, between the coming to dominance of TV as a mass medium and a certain shift in advertising in relationship to changing political, economic arrangements. If from the start "the growth of capitalism has depended on the ability to manage and distribute standardized knowhow and information" (Ewen and Ewen 1982, p. 16), the mass media communication technologies of the twentieth century only increase this dependency. They displace labor strategies as a way to ameliorate economic crises and instead deliver workers to a consumer mentality (Ewen 1976). Increasingly, however, the mass media even refuse the task of negotiating an imaginary relief from the world of production. Once offering "transcendence" over the world of work, with appeals to "family feeling, hunger, romantic fantasy, patriotism, envy, fear of ostracism, the urge to travel," the media now offer more market as the only remedy to the market (Miller 1986, p. 188). This shift in advertising is both reflected in and a function of television programming.

Thus as television comes to dominance, it flaunts its self-referentiality. TV references only its own kind of advertising imagery; it even suggests a certain skepticism about TV as a referential medium of reality. But the anxiety TV arouses about not knowing the difference between the image and the real is also allayed by TV, as long as one keeps watching. The ridicule of all by all thereby promotes watching TV as a "jaded devotee" (Miller 1986, p. 218). Viewers are invited to be childlike, but children are imagined to be skeptical, if not already cynical, about authority. Thus TV not only proposes to dismantle familial relationships, it also seems to dismantle the oedipal logic of realist narrativity. Constructing the viewer as a wise child who need never grow up, TV aims to release the present from the action of the past, offering the viewer only timeless futures. These futures, disconnected from the past and the present, are not composed of scenes to be (en)visioned or imagined as a unity. They do not provide a totalizing viewpoint of reality as cinematic realism does; rather, they comprise settings to be watched. The question of reality is again and again deferred, just as the ending of a TV soap opera is.

If, then, Spielberg's science fiction can be said to transform a movie viewer into a TV watcher, it is because his systematic attention to the father's failed authority in the face of the wise child is informed with an oedipally organized fantasy to disavow oedipality. Thus the home is delivered of familial relationships and transformed instead into a localized site of a mass media communication technology. The TV set is made a home terminal in a global information-processing system of seeing, knowing, and reproducing.

The wired home not only "frees" each family member to become a subject of mass marketing and advertising, it also opens the family to state intervention. This intervention is no longer offered as protection for those cast adrift by the organization of labor, however, but as protection for those cast adrift by the post-1960s "oversexed" family, its members "too liberated" to want to or to be able to care for one another. Thus Spielberg's focus on the disintegration of the family reconfigures the welfare state, staging a conservative response to the demands made on it by women, the young, and homosexuals. His productions create a demand for a reorganized but male-dominated control over reproductive technologies. His productions rearticulate the functions of the state and mass media technologies by figuring them as male-mothering systems that defend rather than nurture only those who seemingly can help themselves. I would suggest, then, that in Spielberg's productions of science fiction, the fetus or fetuslike figure of extraterrestriality is presented as the object of a quest by which the oedipal struggle is situated elsewhere, beyond the home.

SPIELBERG'S PRODUCTION
OF REPRODUCTION

When his toys begin moving in the opening scene of *Close Encounters of the Third Kind,* 4-year-old Barry is awakened. He is not terrified; he is rather delighted. As the camera lingers on his open and undisturbed look, we are invited to see with his look and to watch what he will be shown. We are asked to be with Barry, in the place of the child, mesmerized by toys that come alive, as if in the world of Pinocchio. Barry is driven out of the nursery by the force of the toys' movement, leaving behind his family. We move with him, stopped only by the muffled voices coming from the master bedroom. The sounds, which could easily be imagined to be those of lovemaking, are soon shown to be coming from the television, which has apparently been left on all night. In the master bed, Barry's mother, Gillian, sleeps alone.

If, in *Poltergeist,* 5-year-old Carole Ann naively talks to "TV people" and thus opens up her home to the revenging spirits of the dead, Barry is delighted with the extraterrestrial force that has inhabited his home and made all the consumer products go awry. And if in the end of *Poltergeist* the family puts the dangerous TV outside the motel room to which they have escaped from their home, in the end of *Close Encounters* the male hero, Roy, is described by the scientist, Lacombe, as one who stands for all those who shared a vision and who made the psychic connection through watching TV. Thus, while every TV is powerful, not every TV is a magical message machine, previewing the future utopia. Only the childlike, those lost to TV's hyperreality, can be proper mediums —receivers and senders of information in circuitry with the TV monitor. To become childlike, however, it would seem that the disorganization of the home and the permanent destabilization of the family are necessary. In *Poltergeist* the family remains together, but Barry's family is permanently disrupted by the death of his father and Roy's family will also become permanently dysfunctional because of his wife's and children's seeming inability to share his vision of the future. Roy, like Barry, feels the effects of the UFOs. On the same night that Barry leaves his home, followed by Gillian, Roy meets them on the road, as Roy nearly runs over Barry with his truck. Even though later Gillian and Roy will join in a search, they will never reconstitute the family.

As Roy turns inward, compelled to re-create in drawings and physical models the residue of some image or message left on his imagination by the strange events of that evening, his only true mate or counterpart is the scientist, Lacombe. He too is obsessed with the events of that night, as well as with other events like it that have occurred around the world. The world, represented as a network of locations of extraterrestrial communication, replaces the family as the larger context, against which Roy's lone, inner search is dramatized.

But we first meet Roy before the events of that night touch his life. He is presented to us in the family room of his home, seated with his 9-year-old son before a large table topped with a set of toy trains. He quickly establishes himself as the denigrated dad, responding to his son, who has asked for help with his math homework problems, "I graduated from college; I don't have to solve problems anymore." Then a family argument breaks out over that night's entertainment proposals. Roy wants to go see a Disney movie: "I grew up on Pinocchio and kids are still kids; they'll eat it up." But the kids do not want to see a Disney movie. One child climbs into a playpen and violently bangs a doll's head against the railing. Roy is not merely a bigger kid than his kids; he is not like his kids at all. He is lost in a 1950s fantasy of childhood. Rather than being presented as depressed or in a state of denial, Roy is characterized as the victim of his family's cynicism, the victimized dad of a post-Disney age. The past they deny him and that he will seek in the future is the past of a media-produced fantasy of the family and childhood.

As in the TV sitcom, Roy is derided by his family for trying to be the TV dad of the 1950s who is now a family joke. In one scene, Roy is shaving and his sons come up on him from behind. One hits him on the backside with a Ping-Pong paddle; the other prepares to take a photograph of the father's reaction to the prank, which is, of course, accepting and with good humor. Even Dad knows he is a joke. But Roy is also subjugated to his family's angry disappointment when, after he becomes obsessed with his inner imaginings and loses his job, a painful argument breaks out between him and his wife as the children watch from the bedroom doorway, crying. Finally, his wife leaves him, taking the children with her.

Not only is the father derided by his family, but he himself seems to regress to a pre-oedipality, uninterested in sex with his wife or Gillian, who, generically speaking, seems to be a probable love mate. Rather, we see Roy engrossed with piles of dirt, shaving cream, and mashed potatoes. He finally builds a large mount of garbage and dirt in the family room, seeking to articulate an inner image, a screened memory that disturbs but that provides his only excitement. The actual boy child, Barry, therefore, might be taken as prefiguring Roy's regression to pre-oedipality. The scene in which Barry is taken from his mother into the UFO might be read to transfer to Roy, Barry's position in relation to the mother.

This scene begins with Gillian's observing a strange movement of clouds coming toward her house. She suspects that she must protect Barry. She runs into the house and closes the windows and the doors. But the light and its force comes in from every orifice, invading her place. She turns to close the flue in the fireplace. Counting to three, she reaches her hand into the chimney. The camera switches its point of view to the top of the chimney and then looks down and retraces its own movement as it pulls our eyes up through the chimney from where they were last, at the bottom of the chimney. Minutes later, the act this movement gestures is played out by Gillian, who is in the kitchen. Trying to hold on to her child, she sinks down into a corner, squatting with her son between her legs. He gets away, attracted by the force, its light coming through the pet flap in the bottom of the kitchen door. Gillian runs to the door; Barry is being pulled out head first. She grabs his legs and pulls him back. The camera shoots to her face, in pain, sweating with labor. The sense of movement through a birth canal (the chimney) is here repeated and reversed as if to pit the mother against (her own) nature as she labors to keep her son from being (re)born. Finally, she succumbs and Barry is taken up by the force. Yet it is only Roy's regression to infancy and rebirth to the future that will show what the force means to accomplish.

But before Roy goes in search of what Barry has already found, he thinks of winning back his wife and children. To that end, he goes to the family room to dismantle the mountain he has erected there. He pulls at it, but only after some time does he manage to rip off only its top. Just as he does this, an image of a flat-topped mountain is being shown on the TV. Roy sees the image, and although the announcer warns people to stay away from Devil's Tower, as the mountain is called, Roy now knows what he must do. With no more thought for his wife and children, Roy sets out on his quest.

Although the tearing away of the mount's top has been taken as a "symbolic castration" that "makes possible the [movie's] desexualized ending" (Wood 1986, p. 177), it might also be read as Roy's reinvolvement with and his final disengagement from the (human) mother's breast, making possible man's rebirth, without a lingering dependency on the maternal body, the terror of which is always behind castration anxiety. After all, it is at Devil's Tower that the UFO mother ship will land, replacing Roy's family, from whom he is now free.

Roy meets Gillian again on the way to Devil's Tower. She is searching for Barry; Roy is searching for the future. They arrive at the site of the landing, but only Roy goes up to the ship. Gillian stays behind. At the landing site, there is a trivial interaction of sound signals between the ship and the scientists and government officials who have gathered there to communicate with it. Their communication has been facilitated by the "childlike natives" of Mongolia, Mexico, and India, where Lacombe visited and supposedly learned of the "simplicity" of communicating with "alien others." Finally, the portals of the ship open; Barry and other humans come forth, followed by the aliens. Fetuslike creatures, the aliens descend from the ship, making it appear like a mechanical womb that sustains and delivers fetuses, as well as reborn humans. The aliens take Roy and lead him into the ship. Inside, he stands mesmerized before banks of crystal lights, flashing to the Musak tones of "When You Wish upon a Star," from Disney's *Pinocchio*. The mechanical womb becomes the shopping mall in all its central-court splendor.

Thus Roy's rebirth is back to a future in which the man delivers himself from the maternal body with technological assistance. In getting control of reproduction, the father's authority can be denigrated as male domination is displaced onto male-mothering systems that the spaceship figures and that in the end is seen through the eyes of a group of men only. Dressed in white lab coats, the men stand amazed before the ship, their eyes covered with sunglasses as if to disavow the vision they have made visible, that is, the fantasmatic production of a technology that seems to promise an escape from an oedipal logic by erasing the mother who, by that logic, is required to deliver the son to the law of the father.

Indeed, in *Back to the Future,* the son renegotiates his future by actually traveling back in time to control the events that lead up to his conception. To avoid a sexual involvement with the young woman who is to become his mother, he must assist the young man who is to become his father in winning the mother's heart away from the son with whom she has become infatuated. The son fantasmatically orchestrates his own conception, while seemingly avoiding the subjugating confrontation with the oedipal father or the pre-oedipal mother.

The son gets what grown-ups want, while remaining a child. Thus when he returns to the present, he finds it significantly changed. The history of the family altered through the son's actions, all the members of the family have been transferred from their original "dingy" working-class life-style to an "enlightened" upper-middle-class one. The son does not grow into manhood, he does his father's manhood over. Thus upward mobility is projected as a capacity to put on various life-styles, a capacity in which inner psychosexual struggles seem to play no relevant part and sexual identity does not need to be fixed. Indeed, it would seem that upward mobility goes hand in hand with freeing oneself from all familial relationships. In glorifying the son's detachment from the family that holds him down to (the) earth and to the earthly past, science's fiction liberates all the members of the family for limitless consumption of fantasy.

In *Close Encounters,* then, the control of technology is provided in the narration of one man's quest for outer space, a quest for a "new" time-space (away from the family), a short circuit around oedipality. But the resolution to the crisis of patriarchy this fantasy proposes is always troubled by the threat of the return to the present and the real problems of family instability. In Spielberg's production *Innerspace,* the quest for technological control is thereby figured as a quest for control of the inner space of the family—the prize, the fetus.

In *Innerspace* the government has declared a new scientific interest. Given that the exploration of outer space has been judged "unprofitable and uninteresting," the new research proposed is experimentation in the "miniaturization of man," the actual shrinking of human beings to a microscopic size, invisible to the naked eye. Tuck Pendleton, once a respected military test pilot but now an often-drunk, carousing bachelor, volunteers for the experiment. He is to be shrunk and injected into a rabbit in order to see how he might control the rabbit from inside it. However, after Pendleton is miniaturized, a group of high-tech thieves try to steal the syringe that holds him. During a chase, Pendleton is injected into the backside of an innocent bystander, a neurotic, hypochondriacal wimp named Jack Putter. When Pendleton reappears, he is in a spaceship-type module equipped with a TV monitor through which he sees. He is, however, inside Putter's body. Not only can Pendleton explore Putter's insides, he can see through Putter's eyes and hear through Putter's ears; he can also talk to Putter.

Although *Innerspace* has a high-tech organized crime plot in which Putter must recover a stolen piece of technology in order to return Pendleton to life-size, a subplot involves Pendleton, Putter, and Pendleton's girlfriend, Lydia. At the very start of the film, Lydia breaks off her relationship with Pendleton because he will not commit himself to her in marriage. But Lydia is drawn back into the plot in order to help Putter catch the thieves. She is also retrieved to deliver what is needed to save the plot from collapsing into a meaningless war. After all, without the woman as prize, the image of one man inside another man proposes a relationship between men so that one man's desire for another man's power can appear as the man's desire for a powerful man. It is not Lydia who will actually be the prize, however, but what she has inside her.

Lydia back on the scene, Pendleton coaches Putter in becoming a male hero, suggesting Lydia as an example of the hero's prize. But as Putter actually becomes attracted to Lydia, Pendleton becomes jealous. Jealousy between the men fixes their heterosexuality, and Pendleton is thus free to pursue his quest in the inner space of man. Eventually, he finds what will finally claim his commitment, the prize of his quest, the fetus.

During a kiss between Putter and Lydia, Pendleton, without knowing it, travels on Putter's saliva into Lydia's body. Inside Lydia, Pendleton is stunned by the sight of a fetus, which appears on his TV monitor. Nonetheless, he immediately recognizes the fetus as "his" and realizes that he must now be in Lydia's body. As the camera pierces through the mother's body, her body is (dis)figured as outer space, in which the fetus free-floats outside the space module.

Through Pendleton's eyes, which are inside Lydia without her awareness, we too see the fetus, which takes up the entire movie screen, framed by the space module's TV monitor. Pendleton's look, like Barry's in *Close Encounters,* is offered to the viewer. Mesmerizing and mesmerized, absorbing and absorbed, the look is like a jealous appropriation of what E. Ann Kaplan (1987) describes for romantic videos as the "mutual gaze" of mother and pre-oedipal infant (pp. 95-101). The look is that of the wise child, alternating between the fantasy of being the pre-oedipal infant and the fantasy of disavowing oedipality (and the mother that figures the oedipal threat of castration) altogether. It is the look of the TV watcher.

While Pendleton is mesmerized by the sight of "his" fetus, one of the thieves has also been miniaturized so that he might be injected into Putter and there engage Pendleton in battle. Pendleton returns to Putter's body and defeats the enemy. There, on Pendleton's TV monitor, the skeleton of the destroyed enemy appears where the fetus had just been afloat. The sight of the fetus, a sign of life, is quickly followed by the sight of death.

When Putter finally expels Pendleton by sneezing him out, these fluids are collected to save Pendleton's life. The collecting of micro-bodies, carried on bodily fluids, like the injection of these bodies into a male's rear end, build up an anxiety in the near recognition they offer of the thematics of sexually transmitted diseases. If such anxiety pro-vokes the final scene, in which Lydia and Pendleton are married, the marriage does not fully allay anxiety. As Pendleton and Lydia go off on their honeymoon, Putter realizes that the chauffeur of their car is one of the thieves. Putter gets into his car in order to catch up with the couple, who seem to need the constant threat of the homosexual relationship or the image of the endangered fetus to secure their existence as a couple. Only the evocation of homophobia or the endangered fetus seems capable of provoking a masculine heroics—one that is necessarily supported by an agency outside the family that will police the family, defending it from a "too liberated" sexuality for which the aborting woman and the homosexual male become figures.

If, then, male heroics are both reinforced and relocated in the state by means of the fetus's image, it is because the fetus appears already delivered from the maternal body, as if independent of it. Thus the image of the fetus displaces the mother's body, as the fetus becomes viable through biotechnological, information-processing mechanisms, organ-ized as part of the male-mothering state. Science and mass media com-munication technologies deliver the fetus to life and the family to the seemingly benign womb of the state. The "moving" image of the fetus suggests that the fetus is "alive" as the child is alive. It makes the fetus's movements like those of a child: It eats, grows, and spews out waste material. Thus the viability of the image publicizes the viability of the fetus:

> The fetus could not be taken seriously as long as he [sic] remained a medical recluse in an opaque womb; and it was not until the last half of this century that the prying eye of the ultrasonogram . . . rendered the once opaque womb transparent, stripping the veil of mystery from the dark inner sanctum and letting the light of scientific observation fall on the shy and secretive fetus. . . . The sonographic voyeur, spying on the unwary fetus finds him or her a surprisingly active little creature, and not at all the passive parasite we had imagined. (Harrison et al. 1981; quoted in Petchesky 1987, p. 276)

Both as a production of scientific research and as an effect of science fiction, the fetus is presented as free-floating in space, aided only by some technological wizardry. The image of the fetus evokes a need for technological development. And since that development is, for the most part, the development of war technology, the fetus domesticates war technology, proposing its domestic marketability. After all, ultrasound was itself first developed for the detection of enemy submarines. Signifying the state's future victory in the battle for outer space or international dominance over nuclear technology, the image of the fetus offers immediate victory over inner space—an imaginary recuperation of "a series of losses—from sexual innocence to compliant women to American imperial might" (Petchesky 1987, p. 268).

Condensing the father and the wise child in its image, the simulated fetus rearticulates individualism as an opposition to the maternal body:

> The autonomous, free-floating fetus merely extends to gestation the Hobbesian view of born human beings as disconnected, solitary individuals. It is this abstract individualism, effacing the pregnant woman and the fetus' dependency on her, that gives the fetal image its symbolic transparency. (p. 270)

Effacing the maternal body, the image of the fetus not only promotes the technological wizardry of the male-mothering state, it also marks the decline of cinematic realism, which after all is dependent on an oedipally organized envisioning connected to the thematics of the maternal body. Thus the fetal image also points to the coming to dominance of the televisual and to its collapse of the opposition between the image and the real, seemingly dismantling the oedipal logic of realist narrativity.

But rather than a criticism of realist narrativity, the televisual is more like Spielberg's science fiction, which disavows Oedipus only to relocate the oedipal logic elsewhere, outside the family in the state, where the value of paternity can be rearticulated with male domination in male-mothering systems. Thus Spielberg's disavowal of Oedipus and his denigration of the father's authority only seemingly operate to free the subject from familial relationships. The wise-child positionality that Spielberg's films offer the viewer constitutes what Joyrich (1990) describes as television's "distracted form of identification," "crucial to consumerism" and postmodern culture:

> Requiring the dispersal of desire in order to function, consumerism is TV's only certain value: among the interrupted and open ended texts that constitute American broadcast television, the commercials alone provide resolution, and to the viewer left anxious, bored or distracted by the continuous barrage of images (and fluctuation of positions that therefore ensues), the role of consumer may seem the sole identity that remains stable. (p. 193)

As "the storyteller and ideologue" of "the new middle class" (Kellner 1983, p. 130), Spielberg offers a televisual future connected to a conservative response to the trouble of the nuclear family and the sexual and gender politics that that trouble has urged. If what Foucault (1980) calls "the classed body of the bourgeoisie" (p. 190) was first formed through discourses and disciplines focused on the "hysterization of women's bodies," the "pedagogization of children's sex," the "psychiatrization of perverse pleasure," and the "socialization of procreative behavior" (pp. 104-105), Spielberg deconstructs that body, in the name of a new middle class, focusing on the socialization of the fetus rather than the procreating couple, on reproductive technology rather than on the image of the woman as maternal body, on the immune system of the physical/political body rather than the construction of a homosexual character, and, finally, on the entertainment of children rather than on their schooling.

In Spielberg's self-promoting deliverance of the TV viewer from the cinematic past, the subject of postmodern society takes shape as a wise child, innocent but smart enough to fantasize some time and space for himself in the overwhelming system of biotechnology and information processing, reducing that system to a matter of sheer entertainment. Thus Spielberg's science fiction forecloses the critical possibility opened by the generic exchange between the family melodrama and the horror film. He forecloses the possibility of constructing a critical discontinuity between paternity or male sexuality and male domination, which might make visible how male sexuality is constructed to naturalize certain violent and disciplinary practices of the state.

REFERENCES

Cixous, Héléne. 1980. "Sorites." In *New French Feminisms,* edited by Elaine Marks and Isabelle de Courtivron. Amherst: University of Massachusetts Press.

Ewen, Stuart. 1976. *Captains of Consciousness.* New York: McGraw-Hill.

Ewen, Stuart and Elizabeth Ewen. 1982. *Channels of Desire.* New York: McGraw-Hill.

Foucault, Michel. 1980. *The History of Sexuality.* Translated by R. Hurley. New York: Vintage.

Harrison, Michael et al. 1981. "Management of the Fetus with a Correctable Congenital Defect." *Journal of the American Medical Association* 246: 774.

Joyrich, Lynne. 1990. "Response." *Camera Obscura* 20/21(May-September): 190-194.

Kaplan, E. Ann. 1987. *Rocking Around the Clock.* New York: Methuen.

Kellner, Douglas. 1983. "Fear and Trembling in the Age of Reagan: Notes on 'Poltergeist.' " *Socialist Review* 13(June): 121-131.

Miller, Mark Crispin. 1986. "Deride and conquer." In *Watching Television,* edited by Todd Gitlin. New York: Pantheon.

Petchesky, Rosalind Pollack. 1987. "Fetal Images: The Power of Visual Culture in the Politics of Reproduction." *Feminist Studies* 13(Summer): 263-292.

Rothman, Barbara Katz. 1986. *The Tentative Pregnancy: Prenatal Diagnosis and the Future of Motherhood.* New York: Viking.

Sobchack, Vivian. 1986. "Child/Alien/Father: Patriarchal Crisis and Generic Exchange." *Camera Obscura* 15: 7-34.

Wood, Robin. 1986. *Hollywood from Vietnam to Reagan.* New York: Columbia University Press.

6

ERVING GOFFMAN
Writing the End of Ethnography

> Every sign, linguistic or nonlinguistic, spoken or written . . . , as small or large unity, can be cited, put between quotation marks; thereby it can break with every context, and engender infinitely new contexts in an absolutely nonsaturable fashion. This does not suppose that the mark is valid outside its context, but on the contrary that there are only contexts without any center of absolute anchoring. (Derrida 1977, p. 320)

> Presumably a machine designed according to the proper specifications could grind out the reality of our choice. (Goffman 1974, p. 5)

> We should also be able . . . to program insanity, that is, reduce to a minimum the instructions you would have to give an experimental subject in order to enable him beautifully to act crazy, from within as it were. (Goffman 1967, p. 140)

As if a key to the meaning of "Felicity's Condition" (1983a) that had yet escaped even its author, Erving Goffman begins that essay with an apparently self-congratulatory description that nonetheless becomes something of a challenge to the sociologists who read his writings. "An imaginative

Author's Note: An earlier version of this chapter appeared as "Reading Goffman: Toward the Deconstruction of Sociology," pp. 187-202 in Stephen Harold Riggins, ed., *Beyond Goffman: Studies in Communication, Institution, and Social Interaction.* Copyright 1990 by Mouton de Gruyter. Used by permission of the publisher.

analyst," Goffman proposes, "ought to be able to show the significance of presuppositions that no one else had ever thought would signify" (p. 2). To that bit of the sentence, Goffman adds this footnote:

> A wonderfully hilarious (and sound) example is provided by Jacques Derrida's 92-page analysis of the presuppositions employed by John Searle in the latter's 10-page reply to Derrida's 25-page critique of speech act theory. (p. 2)

Taking up the challenge and the footnote, I want to offer a rereading of Goffman's writings, reworking their presuppositions in order to show how it might be that near the end of his writing career, Goffman found Jacques Derrida's critique of speech act theory hilarious and sound.

The connection between Goffman's writings and Derrida's deconstructive criticism is not easily imagined, at least not at first. After all, Goffman's sociology is usually understood as a criticism of the privilege ascribed to *langue* in the opposition of *langue* and *parole*. Goffman's analyses are often read to privilege speech, emphasizing the importance of speech-in-context for an understanding of meaning.

Derrida, on the other hand, deconstructs the very opposition of *langue* and *parole* to argue that rather than speech, it is writing that is denigrated and then excluded by the opposition of *langue* and *parole*. Reading Saussure's *Cours de Linguistique Générale* as an example, Derrida (1982) traces the exclusion of writing in the production of a general linguistics. Saussure, Derrida argues, rather than devaluing speech, insists on the "natural bond" in speech, "of voice and sense" (p. 44). This insistence is effected by way of an exclusion of writing, which Saussure describes as a representation of speech that perversely poses as speech. Writing is accused by Saussure of simulating the natural bond of voice and sense. Thus writing is treated as "a dangerous promiscuity and a nefarious complicity between the reflection and the reflected which lets itself be seduced narcissistically" (p. 36).

Derrida reads Saussure to characterize writing as having "the exteriority that one attributes to utensils; to what is even an imperfect tool and a dangerous, almost maleficent, technique" (p. 34). By treating writing as such, Saussure protects language from its own capacity to simulate the natural bond of voice and sense. The exclusion of writing thereby allows Saussure to treat the sign as arbitrary, without displacing the subject as the natural origin of meaning. As Derrida puts it:

Only these relationships between specific signifiers and signifieds would be regulated by arbitrariness. Within the "natural" relationship between phonic signifiers and their signifieds *in general,* the relationship between each determined signifier and its determined signified would be "arbitrary." (p. 44)

Thus when, finally, in the *Cours,* Saussure privileges *langue* over *parole,* it is not meant to dissimulate the origin of meaning. Language remains a structure, centered in the speaking subject. Speech is not so much devalued by the opposition of *langue* and *parole*; the opposition is made instead to herald the subject, to stage the presence of the subject around whom the system of arbitrary signs is recentered or naturalized.

For Derrida, the dissimulation of the origin of meaning is not exterior to language but interior to it. Thus, in order both to capture the history of the marginalization of dissimulation and to generalize that history "beyond semiolinguistic communication, for the entire field of what philosophy would call experience," Derrida (1977, p. 317) names the dissimulation of the origin of meaning, "Writing." *Writing* is a critical term meant to rearticulate the absence in speech and experience of the unified identity of the signatory, the referent, and the context. It also names a history of techniques or tools, "the development of the *practical methods* of information retrieval" (Derrida 1982, p. 10). These methods refer to the dissimulation of the origin of meaning because they "extend the possibilities of the 'message' vastly, to the point where it is no longer the 'written' translation of a language, the transporting of a signified which could remain spoken in its integrity" (p. 10). Thus the deconstructive criticism that Derrida proposes becomes identified with "the entire field covered by the cybernetic *program*" (p. 9). Computer simulation presents a writing technology that materializes the collapse of the opposition between man and machine, between reality and the techniques of inscription.

While Goffman's sociology is, for the most part, restricted to holding the opposition of *langue* and *parole* in place rather than deconstructing it, I want to argue that in his later writings, Goffman's analyses of speech are at least suggestive of a deconstructive criticism in which the dissimulation of the speaking subject as well as the dissemination of the context of speech are generally invited. Therefore, I want to suggest that Goffman's writings readjust realism for sociological discourse in terms of the writing technology of computerized simulation.

Rather than seduce the reader into an identification with the forward movement of a narrative, the little examples that Goffman piles up in his texts demand instead that the reader submit to a flow of information, participate in protocols of prescribed sets of behavior. Like the displays of a computerized program, the little examples simulate interaction and dialogue. As Fredric Jameson (1976) suggests, the examples do not serve to "validate" a concept, demonstrating "the difficulties and problems it can be shown to resolve" (p. 128). Instead, the examples show the range of applicability of the protocol that each and any example displays. Rather than representing reality, the little examples demonstrate the working of the protocol to produce a reality effect.

Like simulated displays, Goffman's examples propose a method of analysis nearly indistinguishable from the writing technology or the inscription techniques that produce the example. Thus the little examples not only disregard the distinction of theory and application, they trivialize the opposition of fact and fiction, writing techniques and reality. Like computerized simulation, the examples suggest something like an exact correspondence between techniques of writing and the events, persons, and places made visible as figures of the writing. Therefore, rather than constructing a totalizing viewpoint, as Blumer's writings propose to do, or evoking the empirically real with a melodramatic stirring of emotion, as Becker's writings mean to do, Goffman's writings generalize to sociological discourse what he himself describes as "commercial realism." Taking advertisements as the example, Goffman (1976) argues that commercial realism produces pictures

> in which the scene is conceivable in all detail as one that could in theory have occurred as pictured, providing us with a simulated slice of life; but although the advertiser does not seem intent on passing the picture off as a caught one, the understanding seems to be that we will not press him too far to account for just what sort of reality the scene has. (p. 15)

Shifting the realism of sociological discourse from one based on an ethnography of experience to a realism nearly indistinguishable from re-reading frames or protocols by which experience is organized, Goffman's writings even suggest a critical approach to the analysis of realist narrativity and the oedipal logic of sexual difference that informs it. Thus his writings propose that frames make events, situations, contexts, and persons visible as embodied elements in a flow of action, narratively composed. With little examples such as "the um" of "Response Cries"

(1983b), "the anaphor" of "Felicity's Condition" (1983a), and "the ad" of *Gender Advertisements* (1976), Goffman all but argues that without the narrative fixing of identity and context, speech and situation, the simulation of the natural bond between voice and sense would become more apparent. But Goffman never fully embraces the deconstructive criticism that Derrida proposes. Rather, he fixes sociological discourse with a commercial realism that adjusts sociology to computer simulation while defending sociology from the most radical implications of the technology.

WRITING EXAMPLES

Goffman (1983b) argues that "the um" that we constantly utter, seemingly without awareness, is nonetheless used to manage talk. It allows speakers "to make evident that although they do not now have the word or phrase they want, they are giving their attention to the matter and have not cut themselves adrift from the effort at hand" (p. 109). The um, like response cries generally, brings "information through a message," not an "expression." Yet it is employed just in order to give the desired impression of being an expression (p. 100). As Goffman puts it:

> One has what is ostensibly a bit of pure expression, that is a transmission providing direct evidence (not relayed through semantic reference) of the state of the transmitter, but now an expression that has been cut and polished into a standard shape to serve the reputational contingencies of its emitter. (p. 110)

Response cries propose the indefinite displacement of "pure expression" by its simulation; in impression management, the natural bond of voice and sense is called into question. Indeed, for Goffman, *the speaking subject* is a term, often misleading, that only stands in for a variety of possible positionalities that the "production format of an utterance" offers, such as "animator, author, and principal" (p. 145). The hearer, too, is an effect of a "participation framework," or the "array of structurally differentiated possibilities," that the utterance "opens up" (p. 137). This sense of the production format and the participation framework of the utterance leads Goffman to underscore the misrecognition, in speech, of the subject:

Observe that when such utterances are heard they are still heard as coming from an individual who not only animates the words but is active in a *particular* social capacity, the words taking their authority from this capacity. Many, if not most, utterances, however, are not constructed in this fashion. Rather, as speaker, we represent ourselves through the offices of a personal pronoun, typically "I," and it is thus a *figure*—a figure in a statement—that serves as the agent, a protagonist in a *described* scene, a "character" in an anecdote, someone, after all, who belongs to the world that is spoken about, not the world in which the speaking occurs. (p. 147)

By way of these deconstructions of the speaker and the hearer of the utterance, a response cry, like the um, suggests that an utterance is a "*display*—a communication in the ethnological, not the linguistic, sense" (p. 89). The um is seemingly related to the syntactical or ethnological production of reputation. It takes part in the determination of what Goffman in an earlier writing called "the (in)sanity of place." Goffman (1971) argued then that sanity or insanity is imputed to someone according to whether his or her conduct is syntactically in or out of sync with the situation or whether the "grammaticality of activity is sustained" or not (p. 367).

The um does more, however, than secure the "syntax of conduct." It grounds that syntax in the seemingly natural appearance of the attachment of the figure of speech to the body of the speaker. That is, since the um is heard as the unintended expression of the speaker, its utterance manufactures a seemingly natural bond between sense and voice. Thus Goffman (1983b) argues that a response cry, although a response to "a threat to reputation," is "animal like," as if an automatic or instinctual response to "an obvious biological threat" (p. 89).

The example of um shifts the focus of sociological analysis from the insanity of place and from a perception of misconduct as situational improprieties of a physically bounded place. Sociology is focused instead on the semiotic space in which the subject is imaginatively embodied, an embodiment that displaces the physical body of the subject and therefore is not reducible to it. In "Felicity's Condition," Goffman goes on to suggest that without the work done in speech itself, to naturalize the bond between voice and sense, it would become more apparent that meaning is discontinuous from context and situation as well as from the speaking subject.

THE (IN)SANITY OF SPACING

In "Felicity's Condition" (1983a), Goffman's example is the anaphor. In the sentence "I went to the movie last night but I didn't like it," the "it," Goffman argues, is assumed to refer to the movie. Many linguists take the anaphoric expression as "a substitute . . . for something mentioned in the immediately prior text" (p. 5). Still, Goffman looks again at anaphoric expressions and their antecedent phrases, but when they are distributed over turns of talk between interactants. For example:

John: Last night's movie was good; did you like it?
Marsha: Stop avoiding talking about it.
John: Why, there was plenty of it in the movie.
Marsha: John, stop it; we have to talk.

Whatever "it" refers to, it is unlikely that it is only the movie. Goffman (1983a) offers an explanation:

The notion of an anaphor "substituting" for its antecedent confuses one possibility with a whole function; for what the antecedent does is to allow the hearer to pick out and identify what it is the speaker is making reference to, and what an antecedent provides is a guide to this determination, not necessarily the identification itself. (p. 6)

Goffman not only problematizes the taken-for-granted agreement between an anaphor and its immediately prior text, he argues further that in interchanges or conversation, "one passes by degree from what can be taken to be in immediate consciousness to what can be more or less readily recalled thereto, the *given* changing gradually to the *recallable*" (p. 13). Allusive or laconic phrasing, of which anaphoric expressions are examples, rather than merely representing a state of shared presuppositions, instead seeks that state out. Goffman is arguing that, in talk, the speakers seem to be normatively required to choose just those topics that allow them to speak effectively in minimal terms, in allusive phrasings that only they would immediately understand.

Take, for example, anaphora. Its use is not only a right but also, betimes, an obligation. Speaker's failure to exploit available means for succinctness can lead hearer, and be meant to lead hearer, to look for an indirectly expressed intent, namely, that the speaker is being unserious, emphatic, sarcastic, ironic distancing, overly polite, and the like. So, too, when hearer seems to fail to catch the speaker's obvious intent and responds as though the speaker's words were being taken literally; this also must be read as anger, joking, teasing, and so forth. However, when these "normal" ways of saying one thing and intending another, or acting as though speaker has been misunderstood do not plausibly account for what is in the mind of the individual in question, then a second interpretive step must be taken, and another order of explanation must be sought. To wit: that the individual is temporarily incompetent. . . . Or, if not this, then unhappily that he or she is strange, odd, peculiar, in a word, nutty. (p. 26)

For Goffman, the (one) Felicity's Condition of a speech act is met in being able to demand of another and to respond to another's demand to bring to consciousness. This is what keeps us from judging each other as strange or insane; "behind Felicity's Condition is our sense of what it is to be sane" (p. 27).

But then, meeting Felicity's Condition does not refer to a syntax of conduct, a sanity of place, or "the usual agreement between posture and place, between expression and position" (Goffman 1971, p. 367). It refers instead to a spacing, a timing of breaches—breaches of the presupposed context of speech, of its situatedness. Goffman not only insists that there can be no exhaustive list of felicitous conditions for speech acts, as Austin, Searle, and Grice have proposed, he also argues that the lists of conditions so far constructed, do, however, point to the assumption

that felicity conditions (broadly concerned) and conversational maxims will constantly be breached, causing the hearer to reread the utterance as an expression of unseriousness, sarcasm, understatement, rhetorical question and the like. These "keyings" provide something like a systematic convention-based means for shifting from what is more or less literally said to what is meant, a presupposed interpretive repertoire that introduces much flexibility in the presuppositional basis of reference and inference. (1983a, p. 26)

In speaking, presuppositions and context are necessarily breached as a display of the desire for sharing presuppositions. Any utterance, like the written sign, carries with it the force of breaching or breaking with its context. Thus Derrida (1977) argues that a "paradoxical consequence" of thinking of the meaning of speech as dependent on context is "the disruption, in the last analysis, of the authority of the code as a finite system of rules; the radical destruction, by the same token, of every context as a protocol of a code" (p. 316).

But to say that speakers speak in allusive terms that only they could understand is not to say that speaking is a mere revelation of what is in the consciousness or personal histories of the speakers. Rather, the surface of the interaction, its phrasing and spacing, suggests that conversation is not so much about the speaker's remembering his personal history as it is about his memory being reconstructed in such a way that his personal history is made to embrace and resist the demands of the conversation. If, as Goffman argues, speaking moves from the given to the recallable, it is because speech is structured or contextualized not as a function of memory but to make memory function. Speech calls forth context and makes personal history possible.

If, then, memory is always a reconstruction, laconic or allusive phrasing implies such notions as repression, displacement, and condensation, which register intervals and discontinuities in the reconstruction of memory. That is to say, repression is never completely successful; thus the unconscious shapes the recallable in knots of associations that anaphoric expressions allow to surface in speaking. Thus the objects of speech and experience are substitutes in memory for always-already lost objects, substitutes for loss. To the series of object substitutes, Lacan (1981, p. 53) gives the name "automaton," which Rosalind Krauss (1989) interprets to indicate not only the uncanniness of the substitutes, their aura of actuality, their appearance as if by chance, their just-thereness, but also "the inexorability, which orders the series" (p. 72), what I have described as the drive of unconscious desire. Thus laconic and allusive phrasing suggests that the speaker unconsciously fits himself to the figuration offered by the other speaker, whose constructions are also configurations, unconsciously invested with desire.

As the anaphor points to the phrasing and spacing of speech, it refers (in)sanity less to the physicality of place than to the timing of the breaches of context. The materialization of breaches, like (the spacing) of Writing, always dissimulates the origin of meaning, as the natural bond between sense and voice is shown to be a simulation. The end point and the origin of meaning are indefinitely deferred in speech as well as in writing.

FRAMING AND GENDER DISPLAYS

The shift in sociological discourse that Goffman's works propose, from an ethnography of experience to a semiotics of speech, from the physical body, context, and situation to the imaged (or imagined) body, context, and situation, is often missed or misunderstood. Randall Collins (1985), for example, argues:

> Goffman never succeeded in integrating his earlier theories of interaction rituals in everyday life with his later analysis of frames and talk. But the outline of how they fit together is clear enough. The bedrock of social interaction, the outmost frame around all the laminations of social situation and self-reflexive conversation, is always the physical copresence of people warily attending to each other. (p. 227)

Collins concludes that, unlike Alfred Schutz and Harold Garfinkel, Goffman shows that, practically speaking, people carry on reflexively without infinite regress, precisely because they can always "drop back to the core," to the "primary frame," to "the real physical world and the real social presence of human bodies within it" (p. 218). Collins's insistence that it is the real physical world, or the real presence of bodies in it, that constitutes the "core" of meaning or the basis of what he describes as "the social working of mind" seems to forget that it is the work of primary frames to construct the physical world and physical bodies as untransformed realities.

While the primary frames that Goffman (1974) describes do the work of distinguishing the social from the natural or physical, they are nonetheless social productions, constituting a "central element" of a particular social group's culture (p. 37). The natural is therefore socially constructed. Goffman even implies that it is in the use of primary frames that we see or perceive anything at all.

> It seems that we can hardly glance at anything without applying a primary framework, thereby forming conjectures as to what occurred before and expectations of what is likely to happen now. A readiness *merely* to glance at something and then to shift attention to other things apparently is not produced solely by a lack of concern; glancing itself seems to be made possible by the quick confirmation that viewers can obtain, thus ensuring that anticipated perspectives apply. . . . Mere perceiving, then, is a much more active penetration of the world than at first might be thought. (p. 38)

If glancing is meant to confirm whether some perspective applies, primary frames, nonetheless, inform the glancing itself. Goffman suggests that they do so as narratively structured agencies of perception that place the subject in an ongoing stream of activity, so that "what occurred before" and "what is likely to happen now" can be inferred.

For Goffman, then, primary frames delimit "the natural" to "the purely physical" or "the unguided event," while "the social" defines "events that incorporate the will, aim, and controlling effort of an intelligence, a live agency, the chief one being the human being" (p. 22). Thus the distinction of the social from the natural is always also a distinction that figures the subject as a live agency of intelligence, the origin of meaning. In the application of primary frames, there is always the prior determination of the subject as the very source of the distinction of the social from the natural. But it is this prior determination that is denied in primary framing. Indeed, Goffman argues that if a primary frame works, it is because in its application, the frame "is seen by those who apply it as not depending on or harking back to some prior or 'original' interpretation" (p. 21). Thus the primary distinction of the social from the natural must also involve a disavowal of framing, a disavowal of the determination of the subject as the agency of intelligence, a disavowal that Derrida refers to as the "exclusion of Writing."

This disavowal, I have argued, is operated at the site/sight of the sexually differentiated body. Since sexual difference cannot be equated with either the masculine or the feminine sexes but only with their difference, sexual difference is always imagined; it always fractures any one-to-one correspondence between a particular anatomy and a particular sexual identity. The body, then, is a surface at which perception and projection can never be entirely differentiated; the body signifies the impossibility of distinguishing the natural from the social, once and for all. Because the sexed body threatens the distinction of the social from the natural, it is the body's sexual significations that are disciplined and regulated in securing the primary distinction of the natural from the social in the construction of reality.

As I have already suggested, it is the oedipal logic of realist narrativity that operates to discipline the body. By reducing sexual difference to a crude anatomical opposition, the oedipal logic fixes the natural in the feminine figure and the social in the masculine figure, thereby making the primary distinction of the natural from the social at least figuratively possible. Thus the narrative reduction of sexual difference also allows the bond between voice and sense to appear natural, if only in the masculine figure, whose nature, so to speak, is constructed as social.

In *Gender Advertisements* (1976), Goffman, by way of a discussion of commercial realism, also suggests a relationship between sexual difference, or what he calls gender, and the narrative production of the distinction of the social from the natural in the construction of reality.

Not only is the distinction of the natural and the social treated as a narratively constructed perception, but perception itself is understood to take as real only what is pictured or narratively produced as such. That is, Goffman's understanding of displays of gendered bodies as simulations of nature becomes the basis of his proposal that "the eyeing of live scenes" is "more or less equivalent" to the eyeing "of pictures of scenes," so that "things . . . in effect are as they seem to be seen, and as they seem to be pictured" (p. 12).

Indeed, for Goffman, we learn to see, and in terms of scenes that he defines as

representations, whether candid, faked, or frankly simulated, of "events" happening. Narrative-like action is to be read from what is seen, a before and after are to be inferred, and this location in the ongoing stream of activity provides the context as much as do the models and props per se. (p. 16)

Scenes offer a viewpoint to the viewer by means of an identification with the narrative figures of the plot space, the movement or action. Scenes fix locations in the ongoing stream of activity in terms of an inferred before and after.

If reality is taken to be only what scenes make it appear to be, it is because of the working in scenes of what Goffman calls "the doctrine of natural expression." This doctrine suggests that things give off information that is read by others as "conveying evidence" of their "essential nature" (p. 7). Thus what are taken as the natural expressions of the figures of the scene give the scene its reality. But for Goffman there is nothing natural about expression. He argues instead that we learn to express; we even learn to express "naturally."

Furthermore, individuals do not merely learn how and when to express themselves, for in learning this they are learning to be the kind of object to which the doctrine of natural expression applies, if fallibly; they are learning to be objects that have a character, that express this character, and for whom this characterological expressing is only natural. We are socialized to confirm our own hypotheses about our natures. (p. 7)

Thus Goffman focuses on the display as a simulation of natural expression, the manufactured medium and evidence of natural expression:

Displays are part of what we think of as "expressive behavior," and as such tend to be conveyed and received as if they were somehow natural, deriving, like temperature and pulse, from the way people are and needful, therefore, of no social or historical analysis. (p. 3)

Standing in for the natural, the display is not a "portrait" of reality; it is "a passing exhortative guide to perception" of how things should be seen, how they seem to be or might be taken to be (p. 3). Displays are formal elements of a scene that naturalize the scenic production of perception.

For Goffman, the prototype of all displays of natural expression is the gender display.

One of the most deeply seated traits of man, it is felt, is gender; femininity and masculinity are in a sense the prototypes of essential expression—something that can be conveyed fleetingly in any social situation and yet something that strikes at the most basic characterization of the individual. (p. 7)

Taken for natural expression, gender displays function to frame all other social arrangements; they are the engendering prototypes of all other displays.

And insofar as natural expressions of gender are—in the sense here employed—natural and expressive, what they naturally express is the capacity and inclination of individuals to portray a version of themselves and their relationships at strategic moments—a working agreement to present each other with, and facilitate the other's presentation of, gestural pictures of the claimed reality of their relationship and the claimed character of their human nature. (p. 7)

Gender displays naturalize other social arrangements, especially those of domination and subordination, precisely because gender displays are not natural expressions. Their source, Goffman argues, is not biology but what he describes as "the parent-child complex taken in its ideal middle class version" (p. 4). Drawing on this source, gender displays naturalize relations of power by defusing the coercion of such relationships.

Given this parent-child complex as a common fund of experience, it seems we draw on it in a fundamental way in adult social gatherings. The invocation through ritualistic expression of this hierarchical complex seems to cast a spate of face-to-face interaction in what is taken as no-contest terms, warmed by a touch of relatedness; in short, benign control. The superordinate gives something gratis out of supportive identification, and the subordinate responds with an outright display of gratitude, and if not that, then at least an implied submission to the relationship and the definition of the situation it sustains. (p. 5)

Although Goffman does not answer the question he himself raises as to why it is that it is gender that is invoked in the configuration of social relations, especially relations of power (p. 8), he does at least suggest that there is some connection between the parent-child complex and the hierarchy it enforces as a natural superiority of the masculine over the feminine. Thus Goffman argues that in the application of the parent-child complex, what is usually implied is that "ritually speaking females are equivalent to subordinate males and both are equivalent to children" (p. 5). It might be argued, then, that what Goffman refers to as the parent-child complex is the operation, in scenes, of the oedipal logic of realist narrativity.

Thus Goffman's writings not only suggest that situations and contexts are always breached and that conversation takes place by means of condensations and displacements and the imaginary positions they offer to the speaker and hearer. They also suggest that situations, contexts, and meanings are narratively fixed or scenically organized with an oedipal logic of realist narrativity. It is this narrative logic that is deployed in primary framing.

ENGROSSMENT, SIMULATION, AND ETHNOGRAPHIC AUTHORITY

I have imagined that what Goffman found hilarious about Derrida's sound critique of Searle is that it showed Goffman to himself, on the verge of deconstructing the very notions he made central to the ethnography of the face-to-face interactions of everyday life—situatedness, context, physical copresence, interactional ritual. As these notions are nearly deconstructed in Goffman's rereading of the frames of experience, a question of the authority of the ethnographic observer is also raised, at least implicitly.

Goffman's writings insistently shift the focus of ethnography from a concern with the reality of experience, even everyday experience, to question instead whether "wide-awake life can actually be seen as (anything else) but one rule-produced plane of being, if so seen at all" (1974, p. 5). Facing the "embarrassing methodological fact that the announcement of constitutive rules seems an open ended game that any number can play forever" (p. 6), Goffman concerns himself not with the reality of experience, but with "engrossment," in which what is of concern

> is not an individual's sense of what is real, but rather what it is he can get caught up in, engrossed in, carried away by; and this can be something he can claim is really going on and yet claim is not real. One is left, then, with the structural similarity between everyday life . . . and the various "worlds" of make-believe but no way of knowing how this relationship should modify our view of everyday life. (p. 6)

Engrossment disconnects the experience of everyday life from an empirical analysis. Instead, it connects experiencing to a kind of rereading, the kind demanded of a reader of Goffman's texts. Goffman's texts mean to out-frame the reader, who, in making a considerably awesome thing out of natural expression, can then be shown that what appears as nature is rather social and what appears as social is rather the artifice of displays. As Goffman (1983b) puts it:

> What comes to be made of a particular individual's show of "natural emotional expression" on any occasion is a considerably awesome thing not dependent on the existence anywhere of natural emotional expressions. (p. 108)

Engrossment is perhaps best characterized as a dissemination of the grounds of reality across the material surface of a simulated body, a body in performance, the body of a gender display.

Thus engrossment proposes itself as a rereading of a flow of information in which the representation is not measured against the real. Even though Goffman (1974) argues that "the innermost part of a framed activity must be something that does or could have status as untransformed reality" (p. 156), his examples focus rather on the framing of the "actual" so that whatever that is, its framing, as such, subjects it to further "modes of recasting," primarily "keying and fabrication" (p. 156). Since the "actual" is always already framed as the "real" and in such a way that makes keying and fabrication probable, the kind of rereading

suggested by Goffman's writings is a matter of grasping simulations in
terms of each other, as if a typology of simulations were possible. Thus
Goffman's texts, filled up with examples, propose themselves as constructions of what Derrida (1977) describes as "types of iteration or
citation" in which "citational statements are not opposed to original
statement-events" and in which "the category of intention," although it
will not disappear, "will no longer govern the entire scene and the entire
system of utterances" (p. 326).

Piling up examples, Goffman's texts seemingly dismiss narrativity
and thus disable the narrative authorization of the ethnographic observer. Like computational displays (Nichols 1988), Goffman's texts by
example push narrative to the level of the program, no longer address-
able by the reader, of whom is demanded and to whom is offered immediate, instantaneous response, that is, engrossment. For the reader,
Goffman's texts are judged for succeeding or failing to engross, for boring
or entertaining. Goffman's texts are judged for what Sherry Turkle (1984)
describes for computer simulations as their "holding power" (p. 14).

By pushing narrative to the unaddressable space of the program, computer simulation points to the possibilities of deconstructing narrativity,
but is not, in itself, a deconstructive criticism of narrativity. So, too,
Goffman never fully embraces a deconstructive criticism of ethnographic
authority. While in his introduction to *Frame Analysis* (1974) he recognizes that discussions about framing "inevitably lead to questions con-
cerning the status of the discussion itself, because here terms applying
to what is analyzed ought to apply to the analysis also," Goffman nonetheless proceeds "on the commonsense assumption that ordinary language and ordinary writing practices are sufficiently flexible to allow
anything that one wants to express to get expressed" (p. 11). Failing to
embrace a deconstructive criticism fully, Goffman argues:

> Thus, even if one took as one's task the examination of the use made in the
> humanities and the less robust sciences of "examples," "illustrations," and
> "cases in point," the object being to uncover the folk theories of evidence
> which underlie resort to these devices, it would still be the case that
> examples and illustrations would probably have to be used, and they
> probably could be without entirely vitiating the analysis. (p. 12)

Thus, while Goffman's frame analysis attempts to deal with what
Jameson (1976) describes as "the formal problems of sociological description," in late capitalist society, when the "social material . . . no

longer seems to offer any 'law' or *moeurs* or prescribed behavior patterns" (p. 121), his efforts do not amount to an explicit criticism of sociological discourse or the ethnographic description upon which it depends. Rather, Goffman's writings succeed in proposing a way to ride out the crisis of sociological description, without becoming fully engaged with it.

Thus the criticism of ethnography that Goffman's writings suggest becomes more apparent in the negative assessments of his sociology. As one of Goffman's critics complains:

> The apparent illumination in the reader's mind is based on his unquestioned assumption of commonsense reasoning, evidence and example, and the stipulative definitions of concepts. The reader's impression that he has gained an understanding of previously perceived but un-understandable complex events serves merely to keep him ignorant of the basis of his "understanding" and to keep him dependent on Goffman to provide further "illumination." (Psathas 1980, p. 73)

What is said of Goffman's writings might be said of any ethnography. And now, when what its critics say about ethnography could have been said by Goffman, he ironically becomes the last great sociological ethnographer. And the irony becomes even more insistent when, in the end of *Frame Analysis,* Goffman makes his finale, his own disappearance. With a quote from Merleau-Ponty, Goffman answers his own last question, "And 'oneself,' this palpable thing of flesh and bone?"

> It is not sufficiently noted that the other is never present face to face. Even when, in the heat of discussion, I directly confront my adversary, it is not in that violent face with its grimace, or even in that voice traveling toward me, that the intention which reaches me is to be found. The adversary is never quite localized; his voice, his gesticulations, his twitches, are only effects, a sort of stage effect, a ceremony. Their producer is so well masked that I am quite surprised when my own responses carry over. This marvelous megaphone becomes embarrassed, gives a few sighs, a few tremors, some *signs of intelligence.* One must believe that there was someone over there. But where? Not in that overstrained voice, not in that face lined like any well-worn object. Certainly not *behind* that set up: I know quite well that back there there is only "darkness crammed with organs." The other's body is in front of me—but as far as it is concerned, it leads a singular existence, *between* I who think and that body, or rather near me, by my side. The other's body is a kind of replica of myself, a wandering double which

haunts my surroundings more than it appears in them. The other's body is the unexpected response I get from elsewhere, as if by a miracle things began to tell my thoughts, or as though they would be thinking and speaking rivals for me, since they are things and I am myself. The other, in my eyes, is thus always on the margin of what I see and hear, he is this side of me, he is beside or behind me, but he is not in that place which my look flattens and empties of any "interior." (Merleau-Ponty 1973, pp. 133-134; quoted in Goffman 1974, pp. 575-576)

To these remarks, Goffman adds only one comment, noting, as Derrida might, that Merleau-Ponty only neglects "to apply to these references to self, the analysis they allow him to apply to (the) other" (p. 576). Merleau-Ponty's neglect, I would argue, is the neglect within the tradition of ethnography, to notice that "the other's body, a kind of replica of myself, a wandering double which haunts my surroundings" is figured as feminine to save, finally, the unified subject identity in the masculine figure.

REFERENCES

Collins, Randall. 1985. *The Sociological Traditions.* New York: Oxford University Press.

Derrida, Jacques. 1977. "Signature, Event, Context." Translated by Samuel Weber and Jeffrey Melman. *Glyph* 1: 309-330.

―――. 1978. *Writing and Difference.* Chicago: University of Chicago Press.

―――. 1982. *Of Grammatology.* Baltimore: Johns Hopkins University Press.

Goffman, Erving. 1967. *Interaction Ritual: Essays on Face-to-Face Behavior.* Garden City, NY: Doubleday.

―――. 1971. *Relations in Public.* New York: Harper & Row.

―――. 1974. *Frame Analysis: An Essay on the Organization of Experience.* New York: Harper & Row.

―――. 1976. *Gender Advertisements.* New York: Harper & Row.

―――. 1983a. "Felicity's Condition." *American Journal of Sociology* 89(1): 1-53.

―――. 1983b. *Forms of Talk.* Philadelphia: University of Pennsylvania Press.

Jameson, Fredric. 1976. "On Goffman's *Frame Analysis.*" *Theory and Society* 3(1): 119-133.

Krauss, Rosalind. 1989. "The Master's Bedroom." *Representations* Fall(28): 55-76.

Lacan, Jacques. 1981. *The Four Fundamental Concepts of Psychoanalysis.* Translated by Alan Sheridan. New York: W. W. Norton.

Merleau-Ponty, Maurice. 1973. *The Prose of the World.* Translated by John O'Neill. Evanston, IL: Northwestern University Press.

Nichols, Bill. 1988. "The Work of Culture in the Age of Cybernetic Systems." *Screen* 29(1): 22-46.

Psathas, George. 1980. "Early Goffman and the Analysis of Face-to-Face Interaction in *Strategic Interaction.*" In *The View from Goffman,* edited by J. Ditton. New York: St. Martin's.

Turkle, Sherry. 1984. *The Second Self: Computers and the Human Spirit.* New York: Simon & Schuster.

7

TONI MORRISON
Rememory and Writing

Beloved
You are my sister
You are my daughter
You are my face; you are me
I have found you again;
you have come back to me
You are my Beloved
You are mine
You are mine
You are mine. (Morrison 1987, p. 216)

Given the configurations of narrative authority that have dominated mass
media technologies as well as empirical social science, the question arises
as to whether there is a difference when women write and does the difference in itself constitute a critical deconstruction of realist narrativity.
Certainly some feminist literary critics have proposed a wholly other discursive space, the space of a uniquely feminine voice or writing style.
This style derives from what critics argue to be women's special access
to the pre-oedipal relationship with their mothers, before the imposition,
in language, of the law of the father.

Author's Note: Quotes in this chapter from Toni Morrison's novels *Sula* and *Beloved* are
reprinted here by permission of the author.

In this chapter, I want to argue that while there is a difference when women write, the proposal of a uniquely feminine writing style is a fantasmatic construction of the woman as author, which puts into play an oedipally organized fantasy, a woman's fantasy to deny oedipality in order to reappropriate the phallus for a unified feminine identity. While this fantasy enables a woman writer, it finally fails to be a critical deconstruction of the unity of identity that informs the narrative authorization of realist representation. It fails to disable the reduction of sexual difference to a crude anatomical opposition in the construction of narrative authority.

In what follows, then, I want to reread some of Toni Morrison's writings in order to suggest how they move toward a deconstruction of realist narrativity, by finally refusing the reduction or disavowal of sexual difference. Rather her writings reassert the subject's division in desire and thereby destabilize the authority of realist narrativity. Thus the indefinite mix-up of fact and fiction, fantasy and experience, is restored in what might be described as a ghosted or haunted realism.

Critics, especially feminist critics, have detailed the various contexts in terms of which Morrison's writings are perhaps best understood: "the black-folk" tradition (Gabin 1990), the African tradition (Lewis 1990), the history of the suppression of literature by black writers (Christian 1980; see also Gates 1986), and the history of exclusions in texts written by black authors with white audiences in mind (Christian 1990). Given the various contexts in which Morrison's texts may be read, I would propose that her writings can also be reread to disturb profoundly the ethnographic realisms that underwrite empirical social science, sociology in particular.

FEMINIST CRITICISMS OF
WOMEN'S WRITINGS

In the analysis of women's writings, what Elaine Showalter (1982) first called "gynocriticism," feminist critics readdressed what had been described as the woman writer's assumption that "only the man can stand for the full range of human experience, moving through action and quest to achievement" and that therefore the woman writer "projects upon a male character the identity and experience for which she searches" (Heilbrun 1979, pp. 88, 73). Against these observations, Judith Kegan Gardiner (1982) argues that the woman author (and reader) "uses the text, particularly one centering on a female hero, as part of a continuing process involving her own self-definition and her empathic identification with her character" (p. 187).

Gardiner (1982) insists that the model of "the linear male quest" is not that of or for the woman and that even if modernist texts already break down linearity, "male fiction often splits characters into disjunct fragments, while female characters in novels by women tend to dissolve and merge into each other" (p. 185). The merging of female characters, Gardiner suggests, reproduces in literature what Nancy Chodorow (1978) describes as the persistence in the woman's psyche of the pre-oedipal relationship with her mother. Unlike the male child's radical separation from his mother, the female child's separation from her mother keeps her experience of her self as separate in conflict with her sense of being "overly attached, unindividuated and without boundaries" (Chodorow 1978, p. 137).

But for Gardiner, the relationship between the female characters reflects not only the writer's pre-oedipal relationship to her mother, but also her relationship to her text, to being an author. Women's narratives, Gardiner proposes, are "portraits of the artist in which the artist is represented by aspects of a pair of women rather than by a single individual" (1981, p. 438). The novel about women by a woman is patterned around "a pair of similar but differentiated women," one of which "is valued but defeated, a 'free' personality or artist manquée" while the other "is apparently more stable and socially conventional" (p. 437). The more conventional woman is fascinated with the other, so that the relationship between them is not reciprocal: "One woman in each pair is more of a knower; the other one is to be known" (p. 441). Knowledge of the nonconforming woman usually comes only with her death, when "the questing woman" becomes her "biographer," or at least the end character through whom narrative closure is effected (p. 441).

But certainly the defeat of one character, against which the other's survival becomes reason to make her author of a retrospective account of the other's defeat, is not in itself a break with the linear logic of realist narrativity, as Gardiner imagines it to be. After all, in realist narrativity, final authorization is figured in one character's realizing a "true" or unified subject-identity, the defeat of another character often providing the necessary knowledge for that realization.

What should be noted, then, is that the woman writer makes up a unified subject-identity through the relationship between women characters. Thus the pre-oedipal relationship of mother and child is projected onto the narrative, rather than reflected by it, as the characters come to figure a fantasmatic appropriation of the phallic function for a feminine subjectivity. The relationship between the women becomes a vehicle for frustration, if not rage, caused by male domination, denying phallicity to masculinity. As Kaja Silverman (1988) describes it:

> The pre-Oedipal tableau comes into play only as an after-the-fact construction that permits the subject who has already entered into language and desire to dream of maternal unity and phenomenal plenitude. It is a regressive fantasy, that is, through which the female subject pursues both the Oedipal mother and the wholeness lost to her through symbolic castration. (p. 124)

For the woman this fantasmatic return sustains what Silverman refers to as a "negative oedipal-complex," by which the woman denies any threat of castration, maintaining that only the mother or the feminine subject is phallic. This fantasmatic appropriation of the phallus for the feminine has a positive function, Silverman proposes; it works as "a powerful image both of women's unity and of their at times necessary separatism" (p. 125). It is "one of the governing fantasies of feminism" (p. 125). If this fantasy thereby enables the woman writer, it does so only as a fantasy that leaves the woman (and feminism) yet to come "to terms with symbolic castration and division," "to confront the gap that separates the subject not only from pre-Oedipality and the phenomenal order, but from other subjects, no matter how ostensibly 'similar' " (pp. 125-126).

In my rereading of Morrison's texts, I want to suggest that while a negative oedipal fantasy plays a part in her writings, it is finally worked through. It is this working through that informs a deconstruction of realist narrativity. In *Beloved,* the woman writer's struggle with authorial desire does not end in a fantasmatic construction of a unified subject-identity. Subjectivity remains divided against itself; reality too presents itself as crisscrossed with desire.

BLACK SKIN, BLUE EYES

While it is more a case history of racial and sexual oppression as it affects Pecola, who is raped by her father and who goes mad when her baby and her father die, *The Bluest Eye* (Morrison 1970) also suggests that there is something troublesome about case history, about its narrative logic. Thus on the very first page of the book the text of a "Dick and Jane" primer is printed three times.

Here is the house. It is green and white. It has a red door. It is very pretty. Here is the family. Mother, Father, Dick and Jane live in the green-and-white house. They are very happy. See Jane. She has a red dress. She wants to play. Who will play with Jane? See the cat. It goes meow—meow. Come and play. Come and play with Jane. The kitten will not play. See Mother. Mother is very nice. Mother will you play with Jane? Mother laughs. Laugh, Mother, laugh. See Father. He is big and strong. Father will you play with Jane? Father is smiling. Smile, Father, smile. See the dog. Bowwow goes the dog. Do you want to play with Jane? See the dog run. Run, dog, run. Look, look. Here comes a friend. The friend will play with Jane. They will play a good game. Play, Jane, play. (p. 7)

In the second version of this text, all grammatical markings are deleted, and in the third, the text is typographically reproduced with no spacing between words or sentences, so that the text cannot easily be read to make any sense at all:

Hereisthehouseitisgreenandwhiteithasareddooritisveryprettyhereisthefam
ilymotherfatherdickandjaneliveinthegreenandwhitehousetheyareveryhap
pyseejaneshehasareddressshewantstoplaywhowillplaywithjaneseethecati
tgoesmeowmeowcomeandplaycomeandplaywithjanethekittenwillnotplay
seemothermotherisverynicemotherwillyouplaywithjanemotherlaughslau
ghmotherlaughseefatherheisbigandstrongfatherwillyouplaywithjanefathe
rissmilingsmilefathersmileseethedogbowwowgoesthedogdoyouwanttopl
aywithjaneseethedogrunrundogrunlooklookherecomesafriendthefriendwi
llplaywithjanetheywillplayagoodgameplayjaneplay

The deconstruction of the Dick and Jane primer, of which the reprintings of its text is a gesture, opens to question the relationship of grammaticality, narrative logic, and family "normalcy," all of which appear in the primer as inherently white, middle-class, and strictly gendered. But this initial gesture of beginning Pecola's story with a deconstruction of a primary form of reading and writing is not easily sustained throughout the story, which also draws on a comparison between Pecola's family and Claudia's; Claudia is Pecola's classmate and a sometime narrator. The comparison of Pecola's life with Claudia's reasserts the oedipal logic of realist narrativity, as the decline of one girl seemingly enables the survival of the other, who can then become narrator and author of the other's story.

Thus Claudia's survival is seemingly supported by the good enough care of her mother and father. By comparison, all of the chapters that describe Pecola's family settle on what Barbara Christian (1980) describes as "the inverted figure of Daddy, the older man who molests the girl-woman, and the inverted figure of Mother, the woman who denies her children for other children" (p. 145). While her mother is, for Claudia, "somebody with hands who does not want me to die" (Morrison 1970, p. 14), Mrs. Breedlove, Pecola's mother, rejects Pecola. Just born, Pecola was already for her mother "eyes all soft and wet. A cross between a puppy and a dying man. But I knowed she was ugly. Head full of pretty hair, but Lord she was ugly" (p. 100).

And if Claudia's father is "a Vulcan guarding the flames," giving instruction "about which doors to keep closed or opened for proper distribution of heat," teaching "us how to rake, feed and bank the fire" (p. 52), Pecola's father, Cholly, could do "nothing for her, ever" (p. 127) but touch her with a threatening mix of love and hatred, filling her with a child and driving her mad. Thus Pecola would wish for the bluest eye, having become convinced that only this "miracle could relieve her":

> It had occurred to Pecola some time ago that if her eye, those eyes that held the pictures, and knew the sights—if those eyes of hers were different, that is to say, beautiful, she would be different. Her teeth were good, and at least her nose was not big and flat like some of those who were thought so cute. If she looked different, beautiful, maybe Cholly would be different, and Mrs. Breedlove too. Maybe they'd say, "Why look at pretty-eyed Pecola. We mustn't do bad things in front of those pretty eyes." (p. 40)

If, then, the story of the bad things that happen to Pecola does get told, the telling also informs Claudia's identity with a unifying truth—the truth of Pecola's defeat. Thus, at the end of the story, even Claudia would remind the reader that Pecola's life was used up in "padding" the other characters:

> All of our waste which we dumped on her and which she absorbed. And all of our beauty, which was hers first and which she gave to us. All of us—all who knew her—felt so wholesome after we cleaned ourselves on her. We were so beautiful when we stood astride her ugliness. Her simplicity decorated us, her guilt sanctified us, her pain made us glow with health,

her awkwardness made us think we had a sense of humor. Her inarticulate-
ness made us believe we were eloquent. Her poverty kept us generous. Even
her waking dreams we used—to silence our own nightmares. And she let
us, and thereby deserved our contempt. We honed our egos on her, padded
our characters with her frailty, and yawned in the fantasy of our strength.
(p. 159)

If, in the end, Claudia returns the reader to the text's initial gesture
to deconstruct the primary form of reading and writing, the reader is
also returned to Pecola's wish for "the bluest eye," and to the doubleness
of the desire that it condenses: to have control over (what is desirable in)
the blue-eyed, white discourse and to be desirable to her father and mother,
who, seeing her, would love her. Thus Pecola's wish held within it not
only the desire to author but the desire to be desired as a woman, which
she expresses just after she first begins to menstruate:

"Is it true that I can have a baby now?" "Sure, sure you can." "But . . . how?"
Her voice was hollow with wonder. "Oh . . . somebody has to love you."
"Oh. . . . " Then Pecola asked a question that had never entered my mind.
"How do you do that? I mean how do you get somebody to love you?"
(p. 29)

It is precisely because Pecola's wish for the bluest eye condenses her
desire to be desired that her father, "who loved her enough to touch her,
envelop her, give something of himself to her," nonetheless "filled the
matrix of her agony with death" (p. 159). Pecola's descent is not from
innocence to madness, but from desire to its exacting fulfillment: "the
horror at the heart of her yearning . . . exceeded only by the evil of fulfillment" (p. 158).

The arresting of Pecola's desire in the madness into which her father's
abusiveness plunges her also forecloses a full exploration of the doubleness of authorial desire. But for Claudia's final expression of guilt
over her survival, the deconstruction proposed at the start of the story
remains incomplete, that is, the difference and division of authorial
desire is represented in Pecola but resolved in Claudia's unified identity. A full exploration of authorial desire is all but severed from a realist
account, a case history of the other's oppression. So, in the end, Claudia
can only confess:

We substituted good grammar for intellect; we switched habits to simulate maturity; we rearranged lies and called it truth, seeing in the new pattern of an old idea the Revelation and the Word. She however, stepped over into madness, a madness which protected her from us simply because it bored us in the end. (p. 159)

AUTHORIAL DESIRE AND THE WOMAN-TO-WOMAN RELATIONSHIP

If the struggle of authorial desire is only announced in *The Bluest Eye,* in *Sula* (Morrison 1973) it is made more explicit. Narratively internalized in the relationship of Sula and Nel, the tension between sexual identity and narrative authority becomes the very theme of the story. Thus, while the novel begins with a description of Sula and Nel's community, its history of slavery and racism, the focus quickly shifts inward, to Sula and Nel, who also turn inward, having found that "in the safe harbor of each other's company, they could . . . concentrate on their own perceptions of things" (p. 56).

Because each had discovered years before that they were neither white nor male, and that all freedom and triumph was forbidden to them, they had set about creating something else to be. Their meeting was fortunate, for it let them use each other to grow on. Daughters of distant mothers and incomprehensible fathers (Sula's because he was dead; Nel's because he wasn't), they found in each other's eyes the intimacy they were looking for. (p. 52)

Maintaining the other's distance from masculinity and the blue-eyed gaze of white standards, each of the women enwraps the other in the fantasy she has of herself.

They were solitary little girls whose loneliness was so profound it intoxicated them and sent them stumbling into Technicolored visions that always included a presence, a someone, who, quite like the dreamer, shared the delight of the dream. When Nel, an only child, sat on the steps of her back porch surrounded by the high silence of her mother's incredibly orderly house, feeling the neatness pointing at her back, she studied the poplars and fell easily into a picture of herself lying on a flowered bed, tangled in her own hair, waiting for some fiery prince. He approached but never quite arrived. But always, watching the dream along with her, were some smiling sympathetic eyes. Someone as interested as she herself in the flow of her imagined hair, the thickness of the mattress of flowers, the voile sleeves that closed below her elbows in gold-threaded cuffs. Similarly, Sula, also an only child, but wedged into a household of throbbing disorder constantly awry with things, people, voices and the slamming of doors, spent hours in the attic behind a roll of linoleum galloping through her own mind on a gray-and-white horse tasting sugar and smelling roses in full view of a someone who shared both the taste and the speed. (pp. 51-52)

Each girl's dream complements the other's. While Nel imagines herself romantically, if not conventionally, the bride of a prince, Sula imagines herself the artist, galloping through her own mind. This complementarity, however, becomes a hostile opposition between art and sexuality that years later tears the women apart. When Sula has sexual relations with Nel's husband, Nel cannot understand Sula's actions. Sula cannot understand Nel's possessiveness. Then, Nel becomes like her mother, repressed and rigidly conventional; Sula too becomes like her mother, self-absorbed with her own moods.

Sula is made the "scapegoat, the thwarted artist, the seer treated as a witch," as Gardiner (1981, p. 439) describes the community's reaction to Sula. Unable to create, Sula becomes dangerous:

In a way, her strangeness, her naiveté, her craving for the other half of her equation was the consequence of an idle imagination. Had she paints, or clay, or knew the discipline of the dance, or strings; had she anything to engage her tremendous curiosity and her gift for metaphor, she might have exchanged the restlessness and preoccupation with whim for an activity that provided her with all she yearned for. And like any artist with no art form, she became dangerous. (Morrison 1973, p. 121)

It is only with Ajax, one of Sula's lovers, that she once expresses her gift for metaphor in a prose poem about her lover's face. After this occasion, and seemingly because of it, Ajax leaves Sula. Then, she thinks, "There aren't any more new songs and I have sung all the ones there are. I have sung them all. I have sung all the songs there are" (p. 137). The impossibility of a new form with which to give shape to her desire leads Sula to the one certainty that "a lover was not a comrade and could never be—for woman. And that no one would ever be that version of herself which she sought to reach out to and touch with an ungloved hand" (p. 121).

Like the ungloved hand, the woman is ready to write metaphors, but she does not; she cannot. Heterosexuality is blamed for denying the

woman voice, except to howl in "soundlessness," which is how Sula
describes the only voicing left her when Nel and Ajax leave and there
is only a series of anonymous lovers:

> When she left off cooperating with her body and began to assert herself in
> the act, particles of strength gathered in her like steel shavings drawn to a
> spacious magnetic center, forming a tight cluster that nothing, it seemed,
> could break. And there was utmost irony and outrage in lying under
> someone, in a position of surrender, feeling her own abiding strength and
> limitless power. But the cluster did break, fall apart, and in her panic to
> hold it together she leaped from the edge into soundlessness and went down
> howling, howling in a stinging awareness of the endings of things: an eye
> of sorrow in the midst of all that hurricane rage of joy. (p. 23)

Finally, at the end of the story, when Sula dies, Nel too howls. She realizes
that it was not Jude, her husband, whom she had missed, but Sula. When
Jude had left Nel for Sula, Nel had waited for "her very own howl," but
"it did not come" (p. 108). Now, Nel ends the story with a cry for herself
and for Sula: "It was a fine cry—loud and long—but it had no bottom and
it had no top, just circles and circles of sorrow" (p. 174).

If Sula's topless and bottomless cry carries with it what Margaret
Homans (1983) describes as "a desire to put an end to metaphor . . . collapsing word and referent" (p. 194), it also condenses a desire to erase
any difference between the women in a fantasy of a unified, exclusively
feminine subjectivity. While once the fantasy that enwrapped them gave
the women hope of voice, in the end the circles and circles of sorrow
enwrap them in a refusal of language, a refusal of its old forms. As
Homans puts it:

> Nel's referentless cry closes the novel with an image of women's language
> that radically questions the compatibility of genuine female self-expression
> and the use of ordinary (to say nothing of literary or lyrical) discourse.
> Because it completes not only Nel's experience but the text of the novel,
> as well, its dark prediction applies not just to the individual character but
> to narrative itself. (p. 194)

If at first the women's fantasies suggested that art and feminine sexuality are different, if not opposed, in the end, art and feminine sexuality
are one, as if the woman could speak or write with her body, what some
feminist critics describe as the voiced silence of an *écriture feminine*
(Cixous and Clément 1986).

In *The Bluest Eye,* the woman's struggle with authorial desire is announced but left implicit in behalf of a case history of racial and sexual oppression; in *Sula,* however, that struggle becomes more explicit, as the case history of oppression is left implicit. In both books, the divisions of authorial desire are distributed between two women, so that through the defeat of one woman, a unified feminine identity is fantasized for the other, a fantasy of a feminine body or sexuality that writes. But finally, in *Beloved,* the divisions of authorial desire are internalized within a single woman character. Racial and sexual oppression are also presented, but in a deconstructed case history, its realism haunted.

THE REMEMORIES
OF A HAUNTED REALISM

In *Sula* (1973), Sula's grandmother is punished for killing her 20-year-old son, whom she set on fire because "he wanted to crawl back in my womb and well . . . I ain't got the room no more even if he could do it" (p. 71). So, too, in *Beloved* (1987) Sethe kills her 2-year-old child, but the ghost of the child stays on to haunt Sethe's house, where, by 1873, Sethe lives alone with her living daughter, Denver. Baby Suggs, Sethe's mother-in-law, has died, after which Sethe's two grown sons fled the house and the ghost. But Sethe never thinks anymore of leaving her house. As Baby Suggs once put it, "What'd be the point? Not a house in the country ain't packed to it rafters with some dead Negro's grief" (p. 5). And if every house is filled with grief, so would a woman's mind be filled with "rememories" like the one that often washed over Sethe, about Sweet Home, where 18 years ago she had been a slave with Paul D, Paul F, Paul A, Sixo, and her husband, Halle, and from where she had escaped to freedom.

While *Beloved* is about the enslavement of black men and women by whites, it is also about a woman who, rather than being punished for appropriating godlike powers over life and death, is haunted by her own actions. She is haunted not so much by the horrors of slavery as by the "disremembered," the uncanny return of what is not even remembered to have been forgotten. Thus *Beloved* is a story about Paul D, who comes to live with Sethe and whose love for her drives away the ghost. The ghost then materializes as a visitor, Beloved, who drives Paul D away. Materialized as Beloved, the ghost not only haunts Sethe's relationship to Paul D, she also haunts the novel, the realist account of racial and sexual oppression. *Beloved* is not only about the violent disturbance of a woman's rememories; it is also the haunting of realist narrativity with its own disavowed sexuality.

If *Beloved* is a story of slavery and its aftermath, it could not have been written, Barbara Christian (1990) suggests, "until the obvious fact that African-Americans did have a history and culture was firmly established in American society" (p. 333). Then, in the novel, "language is not only an expression of one's everyday experience but also of those deeper labyrinths of dream and memory, dimensions to which nineteenth-century slave characters had little access" (p. 332). Thus in *Beloved* the African-American story remains a story in bits and pieces, not a unifying memory but the starts and stops of rememory, a reconstruction of a story that cannot be completely narrated, a story that instead makes visible the erasure, the forgetting, the disremembering. As it is written on the very last pages of the novel, "It was not a story to pass on" (p. 274):

> Everybody knew what she was called, but nobody anywhere knew her name. Disremembered and unaccounted for, she cannot be lost because no one is looking for her, and even if they were, how can they call her if they don't know her name? Although she has claim, she is not claimed. In the place where long grass opens, the girl who waited to be loved and cry shame erupts into her separate parts, to make it easy for the chewing laughter to swallow her all away. It was not a story to pass on. They forgot her like a bad dream. After they made up their tales, shaped and decorated them, those that saw her that day on the porch quickly and deliberately forgot her. It took longer for those who had spoken to her, lived with her, fallen in love with her, to forget, until they realized they couldn't remember or repeat a single thing she said, and began to believe that, other than what they themselves were thinking, she hadn't said anything at all. So, in the end, they forgot her too. Remembering seemed unwise. (p. 274)

Beloved does not pass on a history of slavery or of blacks after slavery; it is a story in which the past erupts, tears open the narrative. *Beloved* produces something like what Fredric Jameson (1986) describes as a "case history with holes," "a perforated history" (p. 303). What is characteristic of a perforated history is "something" that "diverts a conventional narrative logic of the unfolding story in some new vertical direction, while working through its elements by way of the mediation of the body itself" (p. 307).

A history-with-holes, for example, is very precisely a kind of bas-relief history in which only bodily manifestations are retained, such that we are ourselves inserted into it without even minimal distance. The waning of larger historical perspectives and narratives, and the neutralization of an older complex of narrative interests and attentions (or forms of temporal consciousness) now release us to a present of uncodified intensities, . . . to loosen our temporal "pro-tensions" and "re-tensions." (p. 321)

While in realist cinema, for example, the narrative flow is often disturbed with the appearance of the body, the disturbance is usually resolved through the fetishization of the body, as the body image, especially the woman's body image, is made finally an object of consumption and narrative control (Mulvey 1975; De Lauretis 1984). In a history with holes, "the reduction to the body and its intensities" is rather "an awakening of fresh sight" (Jameson 1986, p. 312).

In a perforated history, therefore, the visual field is broken up so that elements of the narrative are experienced as uncanny, a haunted realism. What is thereby made possible is the experience of something for the first time that at the same time seems to be already known, known before —what Freud describes as "the return of the repressed." Thus certain narrative elements are intensified so that their historical sense makes itself felt, although their historicity is "undetectable empirically but read off their sheerest formal properties" (p. 316).

In *Beloved,* the realist account or case history of racial and sexual oppression is replaced with a narrative that sporadically is ripped open with arresting descriptions of the body. These descriptions mark racial and sexual oppression without their becoming evidence of the failure or success of a struggle for identity. And different from Jameson's emphasis on *the* body and *its* intensities, *Beloved* gives physical intensity to the man's, woman's, and infant's bodies. There are, for example, the descriptions of the mouth bit that Paul D was made to wear as a slave and the "tree" on Sethe's back, left there by the white boys who attacked her, just before she, pregnant, escaped from Sweet Home:

> He wants to tell me, she thought. He wants me to ask him about what it was like for him—about how offended the tongue is, held down by iron, how the need to spit is so deep you cry for it. She already knew about it, had seen it time after time in the place before Sweet Home. Men, boys, little girls, women. The wildness that shot up into the eye the moment the lips were yanked back. Days after it was taken out, goose fat was rubbed on the

corners of the mouth but nothing to soothe the tongue or take the wildness out of the eye. (p. 71)

"What tree on your back? Is something growing on your back? I don't see nothing growing on your back." "It's there all the same." "Who told you that?" "Whitegirl. That's what she called it. I've never seen it and never will. But that's what she said it looked like. A chokecherry tree. Trunk, branches, and even leaves. Tiny little chokecherry leaves. But that was eighteen years ago. Could have cherries too now for all I know." . . . "After I left you, those boys came in there and took my milk. That's what they came in there for. Held me down and took it. I told Mrs. Garner on em. She had that lump and couldn't speak but her eyes rolled out tears. Them boys found out I told on em. School-teacher made one open up my back, and when it closed it made a tree. It grows there still." (pp. 15-17)

These descriptions work against both the emotionalism of TV soap-operatic versions of slavery as well as against a scientific curiosity, which in *Beloved* is negatively figured in the studies of the slave-overseer, School-teacher. It is School-teacher who, with the ink Sethe makes for him (p. 37), writes each night about the slaves and who also teaches his boys to observe and note both the "human" and "animal" characteristics of the slaves (p. 193). It is School-teacher who even "watches" and "writes up" his boys' attack of Sethe (p. 71).

Thus the descriptions *Beloved* brings forth also focus on different body parts to redouble the disembodiment of slavery and the racism and sexism of "an older complex of narrative interests and attentions." The descriptions show the agony in the body but they do not explain it; nor do the descriptions add up to explain Sethe's life. The reader finds Sethe, her time in slavery and after, in bits and pieces, and never completely. Her past erupts the narrative that insistently tries to be focused on the present, the present in which Beloved refuses to leave Sethe at rest. Thus Beloved is able to disturb deeply the relationship between Sethe and Paul D. The past that he brings to Sethe, in the stories of all the Sweet Home men, is offered, at least at first, as if to resolve his past and ensure a present for himself. Beloved, in contrast, draws out stories from Sethe, always leading Sethe elsewhere, where the present and past indefinitely appear in place of each other, in the space of rememoring. As Sethe describes it:

Someday you be walking down the road and you hear something or see something going on. So clear. And you think it's you thinking it up. A thoughtful picture. But no. It's when you bump into a rememory that belongs to somebody else. (p. 16)

Before Sethe realizes who Beloved "is," Paul D has left. He has left Sethe, even though she had trusted this man, who without trying

> had become the kind of man who could walk into a house and make the women cry. Because with him, in his presence, they could. There was something blessed in his manner. Women saw him and wanted to weep—to tell him that their chest hurt and their knees did too. Strong women and wise saw him and told him things they only told each other: that way past the Change of Life, desire in them had suddenly become enormous, greedy, more savage than when they were fifteen, and that it embarrassed them and made them sad; that they secretly longed to die—to be quit of it—that sleep was more precious to them than any waking day. (p. 17)

He left not only because of Beloved but because this man, to whom women talked, could not understand Sethe's killing her own child. He could not justify that feeling of righteousness that Sethe felt about the killing, about the saving from the slave masters the life she had already once freed from slavery. He could not understand her when she explained that she would not undo "the only thing I had done on my own" (p. 162).

Paul D gone, Sethe is filled with disappointment: "She despised herself for having been so trusting, so quick to surrender at the stove while Paul D kissed her back" (p. 173). With a sudden conviction that Beloved is her child, Sethe clings to her as Beloved seduces Sethe into "the join":

> I see her face which is mine   it is the face that was going to smile at me in the place where we crouched   my face is coming   I have to have it   I am looking for the join   I want to join   she whispers to me   she whispers   I reach for her   chewing and swallowing she touches me   she knows I want to join   she chews and swallows me   I am gone   now I am her face   my own face has left me   I see me swim away   a hot thing   I am alone   I want to be the two of us   I want the join. (p. 213)

But the join only drains Sethe of her life and of any future but death. The mother and daughter relationship insisted upon until the point that the mother becomes the child and the child, the mother, can only turn to silence and death or resentment and refusals of forgiveness.

> Then it seemed to Denver the thing was done: Beloved bending over Sethe looked the mother, Sethe the teething child, for other than those times when Beloved needed her, Sethe confined herself to a corner chair. The bigger Beloved got, the smaller Sethe became; the brighter Beloved's eyes, the more those eyes that used never to look away became slits of sleeplessness. Sethe no longer combed her hair or splashed her face with water. She sat in the chair licking her lips like a chastised child while Beloved ate up her life, took it, swelled up with it, grew taller on it. And the older woman yielded it up without a murmur. (p. 250)

And it is precisely because they judge that it is fair that a mother be haunted by the killing of her child, but not right that the child kill the mother, that the women of the community, at Denver's encouragement, return to Sethe's house to exorcise it of its ghost. Sethe then takes to her bed to die, unable now even to try to convince Beloved that what she had done had to be done. With the correctness of her act, with the judgment of the appropriateness of her self-determination forever held in question, forever held to herself, Sethe is found by Paul D, who returns to her to make her live. He simply offers to bathe her, and she thinks:

> There's nothing to rub now and no reason to. Nothing left to bathe, assuming he even knows how. Will he do it in sections? First her face, then her hands, her thighs, her feet, her back? Ending with her exhausted breasts? And if he bathes her in sections, will the parts hold? She opens her eyes, knowing the danger of looking at him. She looks at him. (p. 272)

And she tells him that Beloved, "my best thing," is gone. He thinks, remembering what Sixo said, when he had once tried to describe his love for the Thirty-Mile woman:

> "She is a friend of my mind. She gather me, man. The pieces I am, she gather them and give them back to me in all the right order. It's good, you know, when you got a woman who is a friend of your mind." . . . Only this woman Sethe could have left him his manhood like that. He wants to put his story next to hers. (p. 273)

Paul D offers Sethe something other than a judgment of her self-determination. He offers himself as a frame for her imagining herself.

> "Sethe," he says, "me and you, we got more yesterday than anybody. We need some kind of tomorrow." He leans over and takes her hand. With the

other he touches her face. "You your best thing, Sethe. You are." His holding fingers are holding hers. "Me? Me?" (p. 273)

In the end, Sethe is divided in her identity: a woman who endlessly seeks forgiveness for killing her daughter but is denied, a woman who would kill her child again. Sethe's is not a unified identity, but neither is she punished or left alone. There is another beside her. There is, for her, the love of this man.

But the love between Sethe and Paul D is no mere valorization of heterosexuality. Just as two women characters may be read to figure the woman writer's fantasmatic appropriation of the phallic function, so too the relationship between Sethe and Paul D can be read to figure two differing stories, his next to hers—the haunting of the unified identity of realist narrativity with sexual difference and self-division. After all, the very last descriptions of Paul D and Sethe are alive with unresolved tensions—the woman in parts that may not hold, even with the touch of the man, and the man's hope to have his pieces put back in the right order by the woman, who may not choose to do so, who may not be able to do so. While Paul D wants tomorrows to come from yesterdays, in the very last pages of the book, there is a return to a lament for Beloved, to produce again the sense of ghostedness, a sense of the subject's otherness.

There is a loneliness that can be rocked. Arms crossed, knees drawn up; holding, holding on, this motion, unlike a ship's smooths and contains the rocker. It's an inside kind—wrapped tight like skin. Then there is a loneliness that roams. No rocking can hold it down. It is alive, on its own. A dry and spreading thing that makes the sound of one's own feet going seem to come from a far-off place.

Beloved.

REFERENCES

Chodorow, Nancy. 1978. *The Reproduction of Mothering.* Berkeley: University of California Press.

Christian, Barbara. 1980. *Black Women Novelists: The Development of a Tradition, 1892-1976.* Westport, CT: Greenwood.

———. 1990. " 'Somebody Forgot to Tell Somebody Something': African-American Women's Historical Novels." In *Wild Women in the Whirlwind,* edited by J. Braxton and A. Nicola McLaughlin. New Brunswick, NJ: Rutgers University Press.

Cixous, Héléne and Catherine Clément. 1986. *The Newly Born Woman.* Translated by Betsy Wing. Minnesota: University of Minnesota Press.

De Lauretis, Teresa. 1984. *Alice Doesn't: Feminism, Semiotics, Cinema.* Bloomington: Indiana University Press.

Gabin, Joanne. 1990. "A Laying on of Hands: Black Women Writers Exploring the Roots of Their Folk and Cultural Tradition." In *Wild Women in the Whirlwind,* edited by J. Braxton and A. Nicola McLaughlin. New Brunswick, NJ: Rutgers University Press.

Gardiner, Judith Kegan. 1982. "On Female Identity and Writing by Women." In *Writing and Sexual Difference,* edited by E. Abel. Chicago: University of Chicago Press.

———. 1981. "The (US)es of (I)dentity: A Response to Abel on (E)merging Identities." *Signs* 6(Spring): 436-442.

Gates, Henry Louis, Jr., ed. 1986. *"Race," Writing, and Difference.* Chicago: University of Chicago Press.

Heilbrun, Carolyn. 1979. *Reinventing Womanhood.* New York: Columbia University Press.

Homans, Margaret. 1983. " 'Her Very Own Howl': The Ambiguities of Representation in Recent Women's Fiction." *Signs* 9(Winter): 186-205.

Jameson, Fredric. 1986. "On Magic Realism in Film." *Critical Inquiry* 12(Winter): 301-326.

Lewis, Vashti Crutcher. 1990. "African-American Women's Historical Novels." In *Wild Women in the Whirlwind,* edited by J. Braxton and A. Nicola McLaughlin. New Brunswick, NJ: Rutgers University Press.

McKeon, Michael. 1987. *The Origins of the English Novel, 1600-1740.* Baltimore: Johns Hopkins University Press.

Morrison, Toni. 1970. *The Bluest Eye.* New York: Washington Square.

———. 1973. *Sula.* New York: New American Library.

———. 1987. *Beloved.* New York: Alfred A. Knopf.

Mulvey, Laura. 1975. "Visual Pleasure and Narrative Cinema." *Screen* 16: 6-18.

Showalter, Elaine. 1982. "Feminist Criticism in the Wilderness." In *Writing and Sexual Difference,* edited by E. Abel. Chicago: University of Chicago Press.

Silverman, Kaja. 1988. *The Acoustic Mirror: The Female Voice in Psychoanalysis and Cinema.* Bloomington: Indiana University Press.

CONCLUDING REMARKS
Social Criticism
Beyond Ethnographic Realism

The other view, coming from a mindset that has been systematically marginalized, may just as well be called "feminist": that the production of public rigor bears the strategically repressed marks of the so-called "private" at all levels. It is not enough to permit the private to play in the reservations marked out by the subdivisive energy of critical labor: the olympian or wryly self-deprecatory touch of autobiography in political polemic or high journalism. It might, on the contrary, be necessary to show the situational vulnerability of a reading as it shares its own provenance with the reader. (Spivak 1980: 73)

In 1986, when I began writing this book, there was a growing awareness, in the humanities especially, that the writings of persons of color, of women, and of persons of postcolonial nations (to name a relevant few) had been all but excluded from various canons that define the value of texts and that discipline reading and writing generally. Thus the effort to open up institutionalized practices of reading and writing to different voices of this society, as well as to different literatures from other societies, resulted from a critical analysis of canon formation—how canonical texts denied authority to other writing practices and how others were represented in canonical texts. Especially important to the growing awareness of the textual politics of canonicity was the understanding of how texts organize their authority by means of the construction of others as screens upon which authorial desire is projected and displaced.

Not only was the question raised as to the construction of an authorial subject, but a critical review of the formulation of history was initiated. Challenging the empirical positivities of subjectivity and history, the critical approach deployed in the deconstruction of canonicity was necessarily dependent on a poststructural criticism of realism. For example, in a decanonizing criticism of colonial writing practices, Homi Bhabha (1986) focuses on their realism; he suggests that the so-called transparency of realism "is best read in the photographic sense in which a transparency is also always a negative, processed into visibility through the technologies of reversal, enlargement, lighting, editing, projection not as a source but a re-source of light" (p. 171). In terms of the deconstruction of canonicity, a criticism of realism suggests that the real is more a matter of the subject's negation made visible in (an)other, a process of substitution in and of desire.

Thus, in the humanities, the encouragement of what is now often called "multiculturalism" fosters attention not only to different literatures, but to a critical analysis of canonical texts for how they reduce subjectivity to a unified identity and history to a totalizing perspective. But it also encourages a critical analysis of the ways those writers long excluded from canonicity may take up their exclusion in their works as their works become criticism and/or compensation. Thus the criticism of canonicity and the resulting introduction of a multicultural approach to reading and writing demands working through to an understanding of all texts as deployments or distributions of persons, places, events, and perspectives in relations of power/knowledge.

But if in the humanities the proposed decanonization of literature was carried forth in terms of a sustained development of critical approaches to textuality, focusing especially on formations of subjectivity and history, no such development has been sustained throughout the social sciences, even though a critical approach to textuality was initiated in the social sciences with the criticism of ethnographic writing. While in the humanities the question has been raised as to the relationship of writing and the institutionalization of literary criticism as an academic discipline, in the social sciences there has been only a restricted exploration of the relationship of social science to disciplinarity, scientificity, and narrative constructions of authority. While in the humanities the deconstruction of canonicity has led to the further development of critical approaches to writing technologies not usually considered literary, such as film, television, and computer simulation, in the social sciences the criticism of ethnographic writing has not enabled an understanding of social science as itself an enforcement of certain practices of reading and writing, similar to those promoted by mass media communication technologies.

To suggest, however, that the social sciences are only a disciplining of reading and writing, as are literature and the other mass media communication technologies, is also to propose that scientific authority is, like the authority of literature and the other mass media, a construction in unconscious desire. It is the denial of this possibility that prevents the social sciences from developing more fully a politics of textuality. It is this proposal that I have tried to develop in this book, thereby to make the social sciences, sociology in particular, turn to face the unconscious processes upon which they depend but that they disavow in the narrative construction of their authority as empirical sciences. In an analysis of sociological realisms, I have tried to bring to the surface what Michel Foucault (1970) describes to be an archaeologically deep relationship between the unconscious and the empirical social or human sciences:

> It seems obvious enough that, from the moment when man first constituted himself as a positive figure in the field of knowledge, the old privilege of reflexive knowledge, of thought thinking itself could not but disappear; but that it became possible, by this very fact, for an objective form of thought to investigate man in his entirety—at the risk of discovering what could never be reached by his reflection or even by his consciousness: dim mechanisms, faceless determinations, a whole landscape of shadow that has been termed, directly or indirectly, the unconscious (p. 326)

For Foucault, both the unconscious and the human sciences arise at the same moment, that moment when man is constituted as a positive figure in the field of knowledge. The unconscious is the limit of the social sciences, necessary to their definition. Thus Foucault also describes the necessarily different if not opposed postures of psychoanalysis and the empirical sciences of man:

> Whereas all the human sciences advance towards the unconscious only with their back to it, waiting for it to unveil itself as fast as consciousness is analyzed, as it were backwards, psychoanalysis on the other hand, points directly towards it, with a deliberate purpose—not towards that which must be rendered gradually more explicit by the progressive illumination of the implicit, but towards what is there and yet hidden, towards what exists with

the mute solidity of a thing, of a text closed in upon itself, or of a blank space in a visible text, and uses that quality to defend itself. (p. 374)

In his contrast of the human sciences and psychoanalysis, Foucault not only indicates psychoanalysis's relevance for the critical analysis of texts, he also insists on the discontinuity of psychoanalysis and realist narrativity. Thus psychoanalysis is not a progressive correction that yields a truer representation of reality. Rather, its difference from empirical science is that it attests to the impossibility of truly capturing the real at all. Psychoanalysis proposes instead that it is unconscious desire that gives a true appearance to representations of reality in defense against the impossibility of truly capturing the real.

Thus the critical analysis I have been proposing in this volume suggests that sociological representations are productions of unconscious desire. Such a criticism is meant to redirect sociology toward constructing itself as social criticism rather than as empirical science. This is especially important now, when it is in "doing science," as Bruno Latour (1983) argues, "that most new sources of power are generated" (p. 160), and when mass media communication technologies can be described, as Stanley Aronowitz (1988) notes, as "enframing" or "defining" all "social construction" (p. 344). Thus, just as poststructural criticism has made use of psychoanalysis to deconstruct the "intentional subject" and thereby to open up to study the construction of subjectivity as well as historicity, so too must sociology readjust its relationship to psychoanalysis in order to provide a social criticism of science and the mass media communication technologies from which science is nearly indistinguishable.

Perhaps among poststructural critics it is feminist critics who insist most on a social criticism informed with the psychoanalytic understanding of subjectivity as a construction in self-division and sexual difference. And it is feminist critics who have noted that even social criticisms that are dependent on psychoanalysis often restrict the implications of psychoanalysis to the notion of psychic or unconscious distortion and its social conditioning. This is typical, Jacqueline Rose (1988) argues, of the Marxist-Freudian tradition of Frankfurt critical theory, but Marxist-feminists also construct social criticism often at the expense of self-division and sexual difference:

> For historically, whenever the political argument is made for psychoanal-
> ysis, this dynamic is polarised into a crude opposition between inside and
> outside—a radical Freudianism always having to argue that the social

produces the misery of the psychic in a one-way process, which utterly divests the psychic of its own mechanisms and drives. Each time the psychoanalytic description of internal conflict and psychic division is referred to its social conditions, the latter absorb the former, and the unconscious shifts—in that same moment—from the site of a division into the vision of an ideal unity to come. As if the tension between the unconscious and the image to which we cling of ourselves as unified subjects were split off from each other, and the second were idealized and then projected forward into historical time. (p. 9)

If, as I have argued, it is the function of realist narrativity to provide empirical social science with the mechanisms of projecting "an ideal unity to come," Rose is suggesting that realist narrativity has functioned similarly for social criticism. Indeed, I would propose that realist narrativity has allowed empirical social science to be the platform and horizon of social criticism. Thus a social criticism that insists on sexual difference and self-division in the construction of the subject functions to support struggles of meaning and contentions over practices of reading and writing, "with no nostalgia whatsoever for . . . possible future integration into a norm" (p. 15). Rather than the "wryly self-deprecatory touch of autobiography in political polemic or high journalism," social criticism would show "the situational vulnerability of a reading as it shares its own provenance with the reader" (Spivak 1980, p. 73). Therefore, refusing a unity of authority and a totalization of understanding, social criticism would refuse itself the identity of empirical science.

If in 1986, when I began writing this book, there was increasing support for decanonization and the resulting introduction of multiculturalism, now there is resistance to both, as deconstructive critics are accused of promoting a policy of "political correctness." Since the criticism I am proposing makes the unity and totalization of a politically correct position the very problematic of criticism, these accusations seem less an alternative criticism than a nostalgia for other times, a persistent desire to return to scenes of an "arrested mourning," as Gregory Ulmer (1989) describes the general denial of criticism in academic discourse: "Academic discourse as we know it has been a mourning in the strict sense—funeral monuments with paranoid fear, internalizing, incorporating the other in the crypt, the foreclosure of a loss, an arrested mourning" (p. 203). Deconstructive criticism, Ulmer proposes, provides a way to work through mourning in the acceptance of loss. Thus he suggests "writing deliberately with the ghost-effect," "not to repeat the past but

to allow it to think in the future, as an artificial memory imbricated with
the living one" (p. 203). Rather than burying the living in writing or bringing the dead back to life in writing, writing should write the dead as ghosts
so that the living can come to live with them.
While only a different writing can suggest, even produce, the *difference* between empirical social science and social criticism, a ghosted
writing, or what I have described as a haunted realism, is not merely a
proposal for experimental writing in the social sciences. Rather, what
is invited is a critical reconsideration of methods and objects of social
science in order to shape a social criticism that can intervene in the relationship of information economies, nation-state politics, and technologies of mass communication, especially in terms of the empirical
sciences.

ETHNOGRAPHY, WRITING, AND
SOCIAL CRITICISM

While many sociologists now commenting on the criticism of ethnography view writing "as downright central to the ethnographic enterprise"
(Van Maanen 1988, p. xi), the problems of writing are still viewed as different from the problems of method or fieldwork itself. Thus the solution usually offered is experiments in writing, that is, a self-consciousness
about writing. It is only when writing is seen to provide the mechanisms
of scientific conception itself, as I have argued it does, that it becomes
clearer that it is this insistence on the difference of writing and field
methods that must be deconstructed if the general function of ethnography is to be analyzed as well as the relationship of social science and
mass media communication technologies. Thus my rereadings of Blumer,
Becker, and Goffman's writings are meant to show that the discourse
on ethnography and its method of participant observation has framed a
larger discussion crucial to sociology, about perception, representation,
empiricism, and scientific authority. My rereadings also insist that this
discussion has always been about writing and reading practices and the
technologies of their mass (re)production.
The ghosted writing of a haunted realism is an extension of the writings
of Blumer, Becker, and Goffman, which, however, insist on partiality
and difference rather than totalization and unity. Blumer's suspicion that
researchers' perspectives will not allow them to see enough for them to
give a complete and adequate representation of the empirical world is

transformed into the positive analysis of representations and the processes of constructing positionalities, tracing the transference and countertransference of fantasy and desire.

If, then, the ghosted writing of a haunted realism insists on partiality and difference, it is to explore the vulnerability of a rereading as a composition of desire. Becker's suspicion that social scientific writers will yield to sentiment is transformed into a positive practice of writing that seeks out the sexuality that urges it, thus forestalling the privatization of desire and its domestic confinement in misnaming it sentimentality.

If, then, the ghosted writing of a haunted realism insists on partiality and difference, it is to stir up scenes of rememory that surprise us with ourselves, who are always already there in the scenes. Goffman's suspicion that social scientists will lose their common sense to endless rounds of self-criticism is transformed into a positive work of social criticism that refuses the defenses and compulsions of methodology in its futile effort to sustain the opposition of empirical science and the seduction and engrossment of all other mass media communication technologies.

The opposition of private and public that has allowed sociology to enhance its authority by making public what is first described as private is an opposition that can no longer ground social criticism. The vulnerabilities of observation become the vulnerabilities of a rereading that, rather than being displaced onto the observed, are returned to the reader and writer. And this is not a matter of urging a fixed identity between reader and writer—only women writing only about women, for example—although this corrective is to be expected. Rather, it is to urge a reconsideration of the privilege given observation and "factual" descriptions as the basis of criticism. It is to urge a social criticism that gives up on data collection and instead offers rereadings of representations in every form of information processing, empirical science, literature, film, television, and computer simulation.

If at this moment these transformations of object, subject, and method of empirical social science can be said to constitute a social criticism that is also called feminist, it is because the feminine figure has until this moment condensed the limits of empirical social science, allowing them to appear as its mastered center. Now, the center no longer holds.

REFERENCES

Aronowitz, Stanley. 1988. *Science as Power.* Minneapolis: University of Minnesota Press.

Bhabha, Homi. 1986. "Signs Taken for Wonders: Questions of Ambivalence and Authority Under a Tree Outside Delhi, May 1817." In *"Race," Writing, and Difference*, edited by Henry Louis Gates, Jr. Chicago: University of Chicago Press.

Foucault, Michel. 1970. *The Order of Things: An Archaeology of the Human Sciences*. New York: Pantheon.

Latour, Bruno. 1983. "Give Me a Laboratory." In *Science Observed*, edited by K. D. Knorr-Cetina and M. Mulkay. London: Sage.

Rose, Jacqueline. 1988. *Sexuality in the Field of Vision*. London: Verso.

Spivak, Gayatri Chakravorty. 1980. "Finding Feminist Readings: Dante-Yeats." *Social Text* (Fall): 73-87.

Ulmer, Gregory. 1989. *Teletheory: Grammatology in the Age of Video*. New York: Routledge, Chapman & Hall.

Van Maanen, John. 1988. *Tales of the Field*. Chicago: University of Chicago Press.

INDEX

Abercrombie, N., 64
Alien, 9-10, 49-50, 54, 59-60
Aliens, 55, 59-60
Althusser, L., 35
Anaphor, 100-102
Ang, I., 69-71
Aronowitz, S., 7-8, 134
Artworlds, 64
Ashmore, M., 26
Autobiography, and realist novel, 67-68

Back to the Future, 88
Barthes, R., 64
Becker, H. S., 8-9, 29, 62-78, 136-137
Beloved, 13, 123-129
Benjamin, W., 1
Bhabha, H., 18, 58, 132
Billson, M., 77
Birth of a Nation, 52-53
Bloom, H., 19
Bluest Eye, The, 13, 116-120
Blumer, H., 8-9, 29-44, 136-137
Brooks, P., 71
Brown, R. H., 1-2
Bruss, E., 40, 67-68
Bryson, N., 22-23

Castration, and authorial desire, 4, 16, 22, 24-25
Cavell, S., 40, 42, 43
Chatman, S., 40
Chodorow, N., 115
Christian, B., 114, 118, 124
Cinematic realism, 35-40; and writing, 40-44
Cixous, H., 80, 122
Clément, C., 122
Clifford, J., 3, 14-15, 26
Clifford, M., 26
Close Encounters of the Third Kind, 84-88
Clover, C., 47
Cohen, C. B., 11
Collins, R., 102-103
Commercial realism, 97
Common sense, and science, 31-33
Crapanzano, V., 26
Creed, B., 54, 55, 56

Dadoun, R., 54
Davis, L., 66-67, 68
DeCerteau, M., 16-17
Deconstruction, and cybernetics, 96
De Lauretis, T., 3, 6, 18, 37, 39, 125

Dematrakopoulis, S., 77
Derrida, J., 1, 94-96, 101, 109
Diorama, 57-58
Doane, M. A., 7, 26-27, 43, 50, 71, 76
Drwyer, K., 26

Eagleton, T., 62-69
Écriture feminine, 122
Elsaesser, T., 70
Emotional realism: and melodrama, 63, 69-71; and ordinary people, 63, 69-71; and the televisual, 69-71
Engrossment, and stimulation, 107-111
Ethnographic realism, and social criticism, 131-137
Ethnography: and authority, 20-27; and cinematic realism, 29-44; and commercial realism, 97-110; and emotional realism, 63, 72-74; and empiricism, 20-27; and oedipal desire, 3-6, 17-27; and statistics, 2, 26
Ewen, E., 82-83
Ewen, S., 44, 52, 83

Fantasmatic, 4-6, 39
Feminism: and deconstruction of ethnographic realism, 10-14; and psychoanalysis, 10-14; and women's writing, 13-14, 114-116
Feminist film theory, and cinematic realism, 35-40
Figure of the spectator, and the gaze, 36-40
Final girl, and narrativity, 47-48
Fineman, J., 6
Foucault, M., 64, 92, 133-134
Frame analysis, and gender, 102-107
Freud, S., 47, 75-76
Fried, M., 24-25, 27, 42-43

Gabin, J., 114
Gardiner, J. K., 114-115, 121
Gates, H. L., Jr., 114
Ghosted realism, 123-129, 136
Gilbert, S., 76
Goffman, E., 8-9, 94-110, 136-137
Goldman, L., 25

Gorillas in the Mist, 9-10, 48-50, 60
Gouldner, A., 64
Green, B., 19
Greenberg, H., 49-50
Grossberg, L., 70
Gubar, S., 75-76
Gynocriticism, 114

Haraway, D., 11, 46, 57-58
Harding, S., 11
Hartsock, N., 11
Haunted realism, 123-129, 136
Heilbrun, C., 114
Hellman, L., 75, 77
Homans, M., 122
Huyssen, A., 53

Information processing machine, 58-59
Innerspace, 88-90

Jameson, F., 25, 97, 109-110, 124-125
Jardine, A., 46
Johnson, B., 12
Joyrich, L., 70-71, 92

Kaplan, E. A., 90
Kellner, D., 92
Krauss, R., 102
Kuhn, A., 35-36

Lacan, J., 4, 102
Lafitau, Father, 15-17
Latour, B., 8, 134
Lemert, C., 29
Lewis, V. C., 114
Life history method: and plain style, 67-69; and the realist novel, 66-69
Lukacs, G., 25
Lyotard, J. F., 58-59

Male-mothering systems, and the fetus, 90-93
Malinowski, B., 15-17

Marcia Lee, F., 11
Marcus, G., 26
Mass media communication technologies, 6-10
McKeon, M., 20-22, 67, 69-70
Melodrama: and plain style, 71; and the televisual, 63, 70-71
Merleau-Ponty, M., 110-111
Metropolis, 53-54
Miller, M. C., 70, 82-83
Morrison, T., 13-14, 113-129
Multiculturalism, 132-137
Mulvey, L., 36, 46, 125

Narrativity: and sexual difference, 22-25, 36; and unconscious desire, 3-6
Naturalist machine, 50-56
Naturalist method, and participant observation, 29
Nichols, B., 57, 49-109
Novel: and bourgeois ideology, 25-26, 68-69; and empiricism, 20-27; and oedipal logic, 3-6; and realism, 20-27

Oedipal logic, and realist narrativity, 3-6, 17-27
Ordinary interiority, 63

Pamela, 72-78
Participant observation: and empirical science, 29-35; and feminist film criticism, 35-40; and writing, 40-44
Penley, C., 5, 11, 55
Petchesky, R. P., 91
Phallic function, and writing, 4-5, 13-14, 19
Plain style, 66-69
Political correctness, 132
Poltergeist, 84-85
Pre-oedipality: and fantasy, 54; and the fetus, 90-91; and women's writing, 115-116
Psathas, G., 110
Psychoanalysis: and feminism, 10-14; and the human sciences, 133-135; and narrativity, 3-6; and oedipus, 3-6; and

poststructuralism, 3-6, 12; and unconscious desire, 3-6

Realism: and bourgeois ideology, 25-26, 68-69; and cinema, 35-44; and colonialism, 58; and commercial realism, 97-110; and empiricism, 20-35; and the novel, 20-27; and painting, 22-24; and poststructuralism, 3-6; and statistical personation, 26; and the televisual, 63-71
Richards, P., 72-78
Richardson, S., 72-78
Rogin, M., 52-53
Rose, J., 4-5, 11, 134-135

Sado-masochism: and computerized simulation, 59-60; and the feminine figure, 46-48; and the final girl, 46-48
Saussure, F., 95-96
Schudson, M., 43
Searle, J., 95, 101
Sedgwick, E. K., 24
Seltzer, M., 26, 41-42, 50-52
Sensitizing concepts, 31
Sexual difference: and anatomical oppositions, 3-6; and realist narrativity, 3-6, 22-25
Sharpe, P., 11
Showalter, E., 75-114
Silverman, K., 5, 38, 39, 40, 116
Smith, P., 2-3
Smith, S., 77
Smith-Rosenberg, C., 77
Sobchack, V., 80-81
Spacks, P., 76
Speech acts, and felicitous conditions, 100-102
Spiegal, A., 40, 43
Spielberg, S., 9-10, 80-93
Spivak, G. C., 131, 135
Statistics, 2, 26
Sula, 13, 120-123

Televisual, 69-71
Terminator, The, 55

Trinh, M., 26   Van Maanen, J., 136
Turkle, S., 109

                                     Williams, R., 25
Ulmer, G., 135-136   Wood, R., 87
                                     Woolgar, S., 26
                                     Writing technologies of the subject, 7-8

ABOUT THE AUTHOR

Patricia Ticineto Clough is an Associate Professor of Sociology and Media Studies at Fordham University, College at Lincoln Center, where she teaches social and feminist theory as well as cultural studies. She received a Ph.D. in sociology at the University of Illinois, where she also studied cybernetics at the Biological/Computer Laboratory. In her writing on both sociology and mass media communication technologies, she draws on feminist thought, poststructuralism, and psychoanalysis. She is currently working on a book on war technology, science, and mass media representations of masculine sexuality. She has served on the editorial collective of *Social Text* and is an associate editor of *Symbolic Interaction*.